THE RURAL
ELECTRIFICATION ADMINISTRATION
AN EVALUATION

By

JOHN D. GARWOOD

W. C. TUTHILL

PUBLISHED AND DISTRIBUTED BY THE

AMERICAN ENTERPRISE INSTITUTE

FOR PUBLIC POLICY RESEARCH

WASHINGTON, D.C.

September 1963

THE CO-AUTHORS of this study are recognized academic authorities in the related fields of public utilities, taxation and finance, and business economics. Dr. Tuthill has been Professor of Accounting at the University of South Carolina and has recently assumed the position of Professor of Business Administration at Emory University. Dr. Garwood, Professor of Economics and Dean of the Faculty at Fort Hays Kansas State College, has previously been associated with the University of Colorado and is the author of numerous articles in learned and professional journals.

Library of Congress Catalog No. 63-21882

Price: $1.00

AMERICAN ENTERPRISE INSTITUTE
For Public Policy Research

THE AMERICAN ENTERPRISE INSTITUTE FOR PUBLIC POLICY RESEARCH, established in 1953, is a non-partisan research and educational organization which studies national policy problems.

Institute publications take two major forms:

1. LEGISLATIVE AND SPECIAL ANALYSES—factual analyses of current legislative proposals and other public policy issues before the Congress prepared with the help of recognized experts in the academic world and in the fields of law and government. A typical analysis features: (1) pertinent background, (2) a digest of significant elements, and (3) a discussion, pro and con, of the issues. The reports reflect no policy position in favor of or against specific proposals.

2. LONG-RANGE STUDIES—basic studies of major national problems of significance for public policy. The Institute, with the counsel of its Advisory Board, utilizes the services of competent scholars, but the opinions expressed are those of the authors and represent no policy position on the part of the Institute.

ADVISORY BOARD

iii

iv

CONTENTS

THE RURAL
ELECTRIFICATION ADMINISTRATION
AN EVALUATION

EVOLUTION OF REA

AFTER THREE DECADES during which the intervention of the Federal Government into the national economy has become an indisputable fact, the fundamental context has undergone a radical change. These three decades have witnessed, without exaggeration, a veritable revolution both in the American economy and in the social order. The United States is today a predominantly urban society, and all trends indicate that it will become still more so, at an accelerating pace. And yet, certain rurally-oriented governmental programs have persisted, and the ad-

1

ministrative organizations to which they gave rise continue to flourish—lending weight to the proverbial survival power of the federal bureaucracy.

The Rural Electrification Administration, born of economic emergency in the depths of the depression, is one case in point. It began in response to a real need and, moreover, in the context of an especially distressed sector of a generally depressed national economy. Today, with about 98 percent of all U.S. farms receiving central station electric service, the original need has been all but exhausted. The economic context, too, has radically changed: barely 8 percent of the total population now lives on farms or derives the bulk of its livelihood from agricultural products, compared to approximately 25 percent just 30 years ago. Yet REA goes on and, from its "home" in the Department of Agriculture, seeks new and expanding areas of activity.

REA is, to be sure, a government agency with roots that run deep in the American community. It has substantially accomplished its express goal of bringing the benefits of electrification to the nation's farms. It commands great economic and political power at the state and local level. About 1,000 rural electric cooperatives are scattered throughout the country, with some 15,000 directors who are men of substance in their communities. REA has a large constituency: some five million consumers of REA-subsidized power have a vested interest in its preservation and expansion. The National Rural Electric Cooperative Association actively promotes both popular and legislative support for appropriations and for the expansion of the cooperative movement into the generation and transmission, as well as the distribution, of electric power. Buttressed by all these factors, as well as by increasing acceptance of the Federal Government's economic role, REA seems by now to have achieved permanent status as an agency of government.

Rural Electrification Prior to 1935

While every other area of the economy prospered following World War I, American agriculture never really recovered from the 1920-21 recession when gross farm income dropped more than $7 billion. The depression of the thirties further intensified the farmers' difficulties. Rural electrification, throughout this period,

2

hinged upon the "market" situation. The distances to be traversed by transmission lines, plus the scarcity of consumers and their extremely low income, meant that it was generally unprofitable for private utilities to enter the farm sector.

Although rural electrification as a federal program was not established by law until 1936, the possibilities of electrification had long been explored. As early as 1878, even before the development of the incandescent bulb, electricity was used to power a hoist to handle sugar beets in a sugar factory. Early experiments in the use of electricity in agriculture were also made in plowing.[1]

During the early years of the 20th century, however, the use of electric power was confined primarily to the larger urban centers. To stay within economic costs, a high-density market was essential. A rural line called for an investment of $1,200 to $2,000 per mile, and as the uses of electric power were then limited, extension of lines into sparsely-settled areas was not economically feasible. In addition, methods and equipment developed for urban use were either unsuited or too expensive for farm consumers.[2]

The first successful utility company effort to take electricity to the farm was in 1898, in northern California, where electricity was utilized to power irrigation pumps, and for similar projects in the Sacramento Valley.[3] A committee of the National Electric Light Association recommended in 1911 that the U. S. Department of Agriculture make a study of the potential use of electricity on farms.[4] During the first two decades of the century, electrical manufacturers were constantly engaged in experimenting with a view to putting electric power to use on the farm. Progress was not rapid.

By 1920, farms were showing striking evidence of becoming mechanized. Some 13 percent of rural roads were hard-surfaced and there was an average of one passenger car for every three

---

[1] *Electrical World*, 1906, p. 698.
[2] Edison Electric Institute, *Rural Electrification in the United States*, pp. 8-10.
[3] C. M. Coleman, *P. G. & E. of California* (New York: McGraw-Hill, 1952), p. 202.
[4] NELA *Proceedings* (New York, 1911), p. 524.

farms. Telephones were found on 40 percent of all farms.[5] In 1919, approximately 100,000 farms were receiving electricity from a central station; by 1924 the number had doubled.[6] Although electricity-producing techniques and equipment were improving, with concomitant lowered costs, it was not profitable for a power company to extend its lines into most rural areas.

Grover Neff, of the Wisconsin Power and Light Company, summed up the dilemma of rural electrification when he noted: "The farmer cannot be expected to use electrical energy unless he can profit thereby and likewise the central station cannot be expected to sell electric service to the farmer for less than cost plus a fair return on the necessary investment."[7]

Even though profit potentials were poor, private enterprise was probing, testing, and pushing rural electrification without any governmental encouragement (or interference) prior to 1935. Efforts were being made by profit-motivated companies, severely handicapped though they were by the widespread depression, to educate farmers to the uses of electricity on the farm and in the home.

Executive Order No. 7037

The work relief measures initiated in 1935 carried rural electrification as one of the categories of relief. It was soon discovered, however, that the problem was much too complex to be handled in this manner. A further impediment was that the government agencies set up to promote rural electrification all but precluded cooperation with the private electric industry.

Until 1935, neither the federal nor state governments had a significant role in rural electrification. In the $4 billion Emergency Relief Appropriation Act of April 8, 1935, Congress included rural electrification as one of eight categories and earmarked for it a sum not to exceed $100 million.

Agencies such as the Emergency Conservation Works (1933), the Federal Emergency Administration of Public Works (1933), and the Works Progress Administration (1935) had emphasized

---

[5] *1954 Census of Agriculture*, Volume III, Part 4, pp. 75-80.
[6] Edison Electric Institute, *Statistical Bulletin*, 1958, p. 65.
[7] NELA *Proceedings* (New York, 1923), p. 45.

grants, grants-in-aid, and subsidies as relief measures. It was assumed initially that REA would operate similarly and would work for rural electrification with the prime purpose of getting money into circulation and the jobless back to work.

In May 1935, President Franklin D. Roosevelt, by Executive Order No. 7037, created the Rural Electrification Administration as an independent agency and allotted $50 million to the specific task of promoting rural electrification. This sum was later reduced to $10 million.[8]

Regulations called for at least 25 percent of funds to be spent for labor and 90 percent of the labor to be secured from relief rolls. It soon became apparent that where skilled labor was needed, it was not apt to be found on relief rolls. Executive Order No. 7130, issued August 7, 1935, freed REA from the relief requirements and made it basically a lending agency.

This order assumed that any borrower capable of constructing and operating a rural electrical distribution system, and legally competent, would be eligible for a loan. Applications for loans came from state rural electrification authorities, rural power districts, existing electric cooperatives, municipal plants, and commercial electric companies. REA Commissioner Morris L. Cooke requested the commercial utilities to submit a plan for bringing electricity to the farms.

In 1935, private electric companies served 95 percent of the electrified farms of the country and, in addition, had the physical facilities and trained personnel to permit rapid expansion of rural electrification if funds were made available. The industry plan called for the construction of 279,180 miles of new rural lines during fiscal year 1935-36. It was estimated that the new lines would serve 206,000 farmers, 79,000 non-farm customers, and add 66,000 customers to existing lines. The average non-farm cost was estimated at not more than $963 per mile. The cost of construction of the lines was established at $113,685,000, of which $100 million would be made available through the Emergency Relief Appropriation Act.[9]

---

[8] Edison Electric Institute, *Rural Electrification in the United States*, p. 46.

[9] H. S. Person, "The Rural Electrification Administration in Perspective," *Agricultural History*, April 1950, pp. 70-74.

5

The industry offer was never accepted, and Commissioner Cooke turned his attention to groups other than those in the private power field, but loan applications were slow in coming. Municipal plants faced legal difficulties and local objections to extending their lines into rural areas. The essence of Commissioner Cooke's policy in regard to the private utilities was summed up in a letter addressed to Senator George Norris:

> The experience of Rural Electrification Administration indicates that this limitation on the extension of electric service in rural areas has been due to prohibitive costs of line construction, to excessive demands for cash contributions from the farmers to pay for the lines which would serve them, to high rates which discourage the abundant use of current, and to the traditional policy of the private utilities of extending their monopolistic franchise as widely as possible, while extending their actual service only to areas which are most profitable.

He then recommended a program of planning on a comprehensive area basis so as to achieve the economies of mass construction.[10]

Rural Electrification Act of 1936

The Norris-Rayburn bill was approved by Congress May 20, 1936, establishing REA as an independent government agency. It had been reported out of committee by a margin of one vote. The chief provisions were as follows:

1. A ten-year program of promoting rural electrification was established with the REA designated as an agency to lend funds to "persons, corporations, States, Territories, and subdivisions and agencies thereof, municipalities, peoples' utility districts, and cooperative, non-profit or limited dividend associations organized under the laws of any State or Territory of the United States . . . at a rate of interest equal to the average rate of interest payable by the United States of America on its obligations, having a maturity of ten or more years." Preference in granting loans was to be given to "States, Territories, and subdivisions and agencies thereof, municipalities, peoples' utility districts, and cooperative, non-profit or limited dividend associations."

2. Loans were to be made "for rural electrification and the

---

[10] *Ibid.*, p. 75.

6

furnishing of electric energy to persons in rural areas who are not receiving central station service."

3. Loans for construction and operation of generating plants or for electric transmission and distribution lines were to be amortized over a period not to exceed twenty-five years. Loans granted for the purpose of wiring the premises or purchase and installation of electrical and plumbing appliances and equipment were to be amortized over five years.

4. For fiscal 1937 the Reconstruction Finance Corporation was directed to loan to the REA not over $50 million with interest at 3 percent; thereafter, $40 million per year for eight years was to be appropriated from the Treasury for such purposes.

5. Fifty percent of the annual allocation was to be used for loans "in the several states in the proportion which the numbers of their farms not then receiving central station service bears to the total number of farms of the United States not then receiving such service." The remaining 50 percent was to be allocated as REA saw fit with the provision that "not more than 10 per cent of said unallotted annual sums may be employed in any one state or in all of the Territories."

6. "Rural area" was defined as "any area of the United States not included within the boundaries of any city, village, or borough having a population in excess of fifteen hundred inhabitants."[11]

Changes in the Rural Electrification Act

Under Reorganization Plan II, July 1, 1939, REA became part of the Department of Agriculture although it still maintained its administrative integrity. Thus, it was hoped that REA programs would be integrated with the Department's overall farm policies. At this time it was evident that REA's scope had not been expanded past the farm. In 1939, REA loan policy presumably still rested on the need for bringing electricity to the farm.

When REA was established in 1935, the rate of interest charged borrowers was fixed at 3 percent, under the authority of the Emergency Relief Appropriation Act of 1935. The 1936

[11] U. S. Department of Agriculture, Rural Electrification Administration, *A Guide for Members of Cooperatives* (Washington, 1939), pp. 43-48.

Act fixed the interest rate at the average rate of interest payable by the Treasury on those of its obligations having a maturity of 10 or more years issued during the last preceding fiscal year.

Effective September 21, 1944, under provisions of the Department of Agriculture Organic Act of 1944 (the Pace Act), amending the Rural Electrification Act of 1936, the interest rate charged on new loans was fixed at 2 percent, and rates on unmatured and unpaid balances of existing loans were adjusted to 2 percent. Generally, payments of interest and principal were to be required quarterly instead of monthly.

In addition, the Pace Act extended the amortization period from 25 to 35 years; and the ten-year overall time limitation of the program was eliminated, thus extending REA's loan authorization indefinitely. The interest rate charged REA-borrowers in a number of years has been considerably less than that paid by the Treasury on its borrowings. In addition, in the earlier years of the program, well over $100 million of REA loan funds were made available from appropriations on which no interest was paid, although REA received interest payments from its own borrowers. These subsidy features of REA are examined in detail in later sections.

Electric systems constructed by REA-borrowers generally required one or more years to become operational. After lines are energized and service started, borrowers may operate for several years before revenues are sufficient to pay expenses and service their debt. The Pace Act permitted interest on future initial loans to be deferred for the first 60 months after the date funds are advanced, with equal periodic payments of accumulated interest and principal for the remaining 30 years of the note. On supplement loans, interest could be deferred for 24 months.

Under such a procedure, REA collected less interest than it would under that of the United States Rule, which applies in all commercial contracts. Prior to the Pace Act, the United States Rule covered REA loans: payments were applied first to the liquidation of all interest due, and the remainder to the principal. Estimates by the Comptroller General indicate that on loans granted in the ten-year interval 1944-54, about $70 million less interest had been collected under the method permitted by the Pace Act.

On June 5, 1957, REA announced the adoption of the United States Rule for payment of interest and principal by borrowers, effective immediately. Under the new policy—which did not affect the 2 percent interest rate, however—principal payments were scheduled to begin three years after date of note except where there was a demonstrated need for a longer period. This change in policy was apparently due to the pressure of the Comptroller General's office and to its critique of REA's method of computing payments.[12]

On October 28, 1949, the Rural Electrification Act of 1936 was amended to provide for a rural telephone loan program. REA was empowered to make loans to existing companies as well as to cooperative, non-profit, limited dividend, or mutual associations for improvement or expansion of rural telephone service. Most of the telephone loans have been made to commercial companies, at a rate of interest of 2 percent with a 35-year amortization period.

Expanding REA Functions

The program of rural electrification has been characterized by a high degree of governmental leadership. Initially there were problems of securing the interest, cooperation, and support of potential rural consumers. Maintenance of the "cooperative spirit" and the stimulation of exciting new projects have been of continuing concern to REA administrators. In 1936-37, one of the conditions that retarded progress in rural electrification was lack of initiative on the part of many farm people, no matter how intense their desire for electrification.[13]

---

[12] Comptroller General of the United States, *Audit Report to the Congress of the United States for the fiscal year ended June 30, 1956*, U.S. Department of Agriculture, Rural Electrification Administration. It is of interest to note, as this study goes to press, that Senator Dominick of Colorado has proposed that all future REA loans carry interest charges sufficient to cover the Government's cost—i.e., at a rate not less than that paid on the Treasury's marketable securities with a comparable maturity date, plus one-half of 1 percent for administrative expenses. Senators Lausche and Bennett and Representative Teague (California) have also introduced legislation which would have substantially the same effect—in addition to other provisions discussed below, pp. 57-58.

[13] Person, *op. cit.*, p. 78.

9

Almost from the beginning, REA personnel have provided guidance to the whole electrification process. REA led the fight to see to it that, on a state basis, there was a salutary legal climate for the formation of cooperatives. Shortly after REA's establishment, new functional segments were added to its organization—a utilization division that advised a potential applicant of the advantages of electricity; a division to aid the applicant in applying for a loan; an engineering division to aid in cost estimation in design and construction; a staff to handle the legal problems of borrowers; and an operations division to aid in building co-op membership and developing membership morale.[14]

The divisions of REA have been more minutely compartmentalized as REA functions have expanded over the years. There is no step in the electrification process which has not been guided by REA directives in one way or another. Thus, "production control has been brought to a higher effectiveness through production control devices and meetings under the personal attention of the Deputy Administrator. Know-how procedures and controls, developed basically in 1937-39 and refined through subsequent years, had by 1945 freed top administration of REA, facing postwar problems, for more attention to matters of long-run and fundamental significance."[15]

Specialists and technicians—through the media of field visits, operating memoranda, bulletins, conferences of system superintendents, meetings of system officials and members, and extensive correspondence—mold and mesh rural electrification activities the country over.

Thus, although REA Bulletin 2-1R1, issued June 8, 1950, notes that each borrower is an independent corporate body responsible for its own affairs and that as the borrower gains in experience and maturity the advice and assistance of REA shall progressively diminish, there is some question as to whether this actually takes place. It seems likely that the area of decision-making by REA changes as the borrower stabilizes, but the basic decisions are still Washington-oriented. It is in this way that unity of "strategic" policymaking is achieved. Once established, many

---

[14] *Ibid.*, pp. 70-89.
[15] *Ibid.*, p. 83.

10

"tactical" decisions may then be left to local decision-making. In 1953, in order to mesh REA loaning policy with that of the Department of Agriculture, another Reorganization Act was passed which gave the Secretary of Agriculture authority over the loan-making power of the REA Administrator. The REA Administrator is now required to clear all loans of $500,000 and over with the Secretary's office.

The National Rural Electric Cooperative Association

One of the features of REA growth has been the increased importance of the National Rural Electric Cooperative Association as a policymaking body for rural cooperatives. Organized in 1942, the NRECA by 1960 had in its membership 93 percent of all rural electric cooperative systems in the United States— 958 systems in 46 states. It is a self-styled "non-partisan, non-profit, private service organization of rural electric cooperatives, public power districts, and public utility districts."[16]

The Task Force report on Lending Agencies prepared for the Commission on Organization of the Executive Branch of the Government (the second Hoover Commission), in appraising the activities of the NRECA, noted that:

> At the present time, this Association welds the local cooperatives into a unified political group and devotes much of its effort toward political ends. It supplies the cooperatives with information and encourages their interest in and solicits their support for the national aspects of the program as they are interpreted by its professional staff. The staff acts as promoter and lobbyist for the program. According to the professional staff people, it is the Association's acknowledged view, and that of its members, that REA co-ops are in free economic competition with investor-owned power companies not assisted by the Government, and it is the aim of the Association to gain for the co-ops and their members every competitive advantage that is possible within the framework of the program.

> An example of the aims and work of the Association occurred recently when the 1955 budget of REA was considered by the Congress. Officials of the REA had assessed its needs and asked for $50 million to make new loans in fiscal 1955. During its consideration of this request Congress was advised by the National Rural Electric Cooperative Association that the Administration's request was not sufficient. There should be additional funds, it was argued, to make it possible for some of the co-ops to initiate negotiations for the erection of generator facilities and transmission lines so that the systems served could generate their own power and transmit it to the distribution centers.

[16] NRECA, *Rural Electric Fact Book* (Washington, 1960), p. 43.

The record shows, however, that the erection of generation facilities and transmission lines was not actually contemplated by the REA co-ops. . . . The amount requested by REA was $50 million; the amount of the revised Congressional appropriations was $135 million.[17]

Current Modifications of REA Policy

REA has undergone a significant metamorphosis in its policies and programs since 1935. Although originally designed to lend money to electrify farms not receiving central station service, by 1961 it was primarily financing the development of an integrated rural power system organized and operated through cooperatives.

In the first 25 years of the rural electrification program, electrified farms in the U. S. increased from about 10.9 percent to 96.8 percent of total farms, and it should be noted that over half the nation's farms are now served by REA-financed systems. Thus, of 6,812,350 farms as of January 1935, 743,959 or 10.9 percent were receiving central station service; April 1, 1940, of 6,096,799 farms, 1,853,249 or 30.4 percent were receiving central station service; April 1, 1950, of 5,382,134 farms, 4,154,359 or 77.2 percent were receiving central station service; June 30, 1962, of 3,818,200 farms, 3,726,850 or 97.6 percent were receiving central station electric service.[18]

REA-borrowers also serve a large number of non-farm rural residences, schools, churches, business establishments, and industrial plants. By 1960, more than 4.8 million consumers in 46 states, the Virgin Islands, and Puerto Rico received electricity from REA-borrowers.[19] The total now exceeds 5 million.

Table I indicates the number of borrowers for selected years, 1936 through 1960, as well as miles energized, while Table II shows consumers served by REA. It will be noted that consumers have about tripled in number since World War II.

---

[17] Commission on Organization of the Executive Branch of the Government, Task Force on Lending Agencies, *Lending Agencies*, February 1955, pp. 66-67.

[18] U.S. Department of Agriculture, Rural Electrification Administration, *Report of the Administrator*, 1962, p. 16.

[19] U.S. Department of Agriculture, Rural Electrification Administration, *Report of the Administrator*, 1960, p. 2.

Among the changes that have taken place in the REA program, two in particular have far-reaching implications for the power industry: (1) the increased numbers of non-farm users of electricity in the REA program, i.e., the change in the nature

Table I
NUMBER OF BORROWERS AND MILES ENERGIZED

| As of | Number of borrowers | | | Miles energized | | |
	Total	Active	Loan repaid	Total	By active borrowers	By loan repaid borrowers
June 30, 1960....	1,034	978	56	1,454,081	1,439,219	14,862
June 30, 1959....	1,031	975	56	1,437,073	1,422,211	14,862
June 30, 1958....	1,030	975	55	1,414,034	1,399,100	14,934
June 30, 1956....	1,026	980	46	1,372,001	1,360,784	11,217
June 30, 1954....	1,022	981	41	1,315,630	1,306,169	9,461
June 30, 1952....	1,016	980	36	1,210,473	1,202,640	7,833
June 30, 1950....	999	970	29	1,018,336	1,012,616	5,720
June 30, 1948....	931	907	24	666,156	661,261	4,895
June 30, 1946....	856	842	14	474,907	470,992	3,915
June 30; 1944....	815	808	7	397,861	395,438	2,423
June 30, 1942....	789	785	4	369,129	368,365	764
June 30, 1940....	630	629	1	232,978	232,886	92
June 30, 1938....	248	248	0	41,736	41,736	....
June 30, 1936....	11	11	0	400	400	....

Source: U. S. Department of Agriculture, Rural Electrification Administration, "Statistics of REA Borrowers with Energized Systems, Rural Electrification Program," *Quarterly Statistical Summary,* December 1960.

Table II
CONSUMERS SERVED

As of	Total	By active borrowers	By loan repaid borrowers
June 30, 1960..............................	4,766,931	4,696,188	70,743
June 30, 1959..............................	4,653,502	4,582,759	70,743
June 30, 1958..............................	4,521,997	4,450,385	71,612
June 30, 1956..............................	4,301,705	4,251,476	50,229
June 30, 1954..............................	4,109,223	4,066,302	42,921
June 30, 1952..............................	3,769,426	3,735,435	33,991
June 30, 1950..............................	3,251,787	3,227,783	24,004
J'·ne 30, 1948..............................	2,263,869	2,243,²56	20 ⁶13
June 30, 1946..............................	1,549,057	1,533,584	15,473
June 30, 1944..............................	1,152,031	1,141,130	10,901
June 30, 1942..............................	981,193	978,393	2,800
June 30, 1940..............................	549,604	549,238	366
June 30, 1938..............................	104,528	104,528	....
June 30, 1936..............................	693	693	....

Source: U. S. Department of Agriculture, Rural Electrification Administration, "Statistics of REA Borrowers with Energized Systems, Rural Electrification Program," *Quarterly Statistical Summary,* December 1960.

of REA customers; and (2) the increased importance of generating and transmission loans, i.e., the change in the nature of the service rendered by REA-borrowers.

During the first few years of the program, over 80 percent of the customers of REA-borrowers were farms. Today, almost 50 percent of the customers are non-farm, and three out of every four new electric services being added to REA lines are for non-farm customers. In 1959, 48 percent of the revenues received by distribution came from sales of electric energy to farm consumers, 28 percent to non-farm residential, 11 percent to commercial and small power consumer, 8 percent to large power consumer, and 5 percent to others.[20]

Although as of June 30, 1962, 97.6 percent of farms were receiving central station electric service, the number of REA loans outstanding is steadily growing. In 1961 alone, loan funds advanced approximated $220 million.[21]

The REA Act, as amended, permits REA to make loans to serve any customer in rural areas not receiving central service. Rural areas are defined in the law as being not within the boundaries of a city, village, or borough having a population in excess of 1,500, and "such a term shall be deemed to include both the farm and non-farm population thereof." Although the law was enacted primarily to bring electricity to farms, there is nothing in the law that in any way restricts REA-borrowers from serving non-farm customers in "rural" areas.

REA has made about 93 percent of its electrification loans to cooperatives organized under state laws. As of July 1, 1961, REA had approved about $4.4 billion in loans to 1,089 borrowers. These borrowers included 986 cooperatives, 51 public power districts, 28 other public bodies, and 24 electric companies.[22]

---

[20] Rural Electrification Administration, *Annual Statistical Report*, August 1960, p. XV.

[21] 87th Congress, 1st Session, *Department of Agriculture Appropriations for 1962*, Hearings before the House Subcommittee on Appropriations, p. 451.

[22] U. S. Department of Agriculture, Rural Electrification Administration, *The REA Rural Electrification Loan Program in the United States*, 1961, p. 2.

14

Table III summarizes the loans approved by purpose from 1935 through June 30, 1961. In fiscal year 1961, about 55.3 percent of all REA loans authorized were for generating and transmission purposes. In fiscal year 1960, it was about 40.4 percent; in 1959, about 34 percent. For fiscal year 1962, the estimate is 57 percent.

Table III

LOANS APPROVED BY PURPOSE

Total loans approved (rescissions deducted)

As of	Distribution systems	Generation and transmission	Consumer facilities
June 30, 1961	$3,267,671,652	$1,113,465,903	$43,618,853
June 30, 1960	3,147,093,575	963,966,804	42,265,372
June 30, 1959	3,016,489,991	885,281,913	40,566,635
June 30, 1958	2,909,046,859	825,370,088	38,160,705
June 30, 1957	2,757,430,954	744,832,130	34,692,344
June 30, 1956	2,581,617,628	626,879,209	29,753,922
June 30, 1955	2,456,908,154	567,707,219	25,504,041
June 30, 1954	2,334,610,711	529,507,230	21,814,158
June 30, 1953	2,202,040,705	507,749,760	20,238,620
June 30, 1952	2,079,914,942	490,136,937	20,578,046
June 30, 1951	1,977,548,012	428,749,956	20,506,146
June 30, 1950	1,811,920,187	377,591,325	15,958,802
June 30, 1949	1,575,057,155	241,152,115	14,109,588
June 30, 1948	1,211,671,584	156,151,589	13,636,088
June 30, 1947	939,013,815	116,173,556	13,248,791
June 30, 1946	781,445,466	82,843,661	12,625,863
May 11, 1935 through June 30, 1945	461,859,421	50,923,618	11,759,463

Source: U. S. Department of Agriculture, Rural Electrification Administration, *Monthly Statistical Summary*, No. 244, August 1961.

The proportion of loan funds used for generating and transmission has increased tremendously over the years. From REA's inception in 1935 through fiscal year 1941, only about 3 percent of all loan funds were for such purposes. From 1946 through 1950, the total rose to 19 percent, and from 1954 through fiscal year 1959, it was 31 percent. As a consequence, it is not surprising that the proportion of all electric power consumed by REA systems which was furnished by REA-borrowers rose from 7.7 percent in 1941 to 15.8 percent in 1958.

When the House Committee on Interstate and Foreign Commerce was considering the original REA Act in 1936, the first Administrator of that agency, Morris L. Cooke, told the Com-

15

mittee: "In 99 instances out of 100 they are going to buy current from existing plants." Thus, he was implying that in most instances REA loans would not be used to build generation plants.

During the course of the Senate debate in February 1936, Senator Norris, the author of the Senate bill, read a memorandum of Mr. Cooke's relative to prospective policy concerning generating loans. He said that loans could be made for such purposes "but we must be shown conclusively: (1) that energy is not available from any existing source; (2) that the proposed generating plant can produce energy at a lower cost than it could be obtained from any other source; (3) that the output of such plant will be used mainly for supplying energy for use in rural areas."[23]

Hence, from the outset it was accepted that such loans could be made—but within specified guidelines. The REA Annual Report for 1939 states: "The REA has repeatedly demonstrated its willingness to allot funds for a cooperative power plant where a borrower could not obtain power at reasonable rates, as well as where no other source of power existed."[24]

In December 1946, under Administrator Wickard, this policy with respect to loans for generation and transmission facilities was substantially reaffirmed.[25]

REA Bulletin 20-6, issued May 31, 1961, added a third category to the two noted above. Loans for construction of generation and transmission facilities will now be made "where generation and transmission facilities are necessary to protect the security and effectiveness of REA-financed systems."

Thus, at the present time there are three broad criteria for granting loans to finance the construction of generation and transmission facilities. They are subject to such varied interpretation, however, that they open wide vistas for the promotion of ever-expanding REA projects—requiring ever-increasing federal outlays.

---

[23] *Congressional Record,* 74th Congress, 2d Session, p. 2823.
[24] *1939 Report of Rural Electrification Administration,* p. 85.
[25] United States Department of Agriculture, *Report of the Administrator of the Rural Electrification Administration,* 1946, p. 25.

REA Future Policy

REA Administrator Norman M. Clapp, who took office in March 1961, has indicated that REA loan activity will be stepped up still further. He stated future REA policy very clearly in his 1961 addresses to various regional meetings of the National Rural Electric Cooperative Association and to other groups concerned with rural electrification.

Briefly, Mr. Clapp's projection for REA includes an enlarged capacity for REA-borrowers to make loans; increased use of the third category for the granting of generation and transmission loans, for the "security" of the system; the establishment of electrical cooperatives on a permanent basis in the electric power industry as well as the use of interregional transmission ties in the hydropower field; promotion of power systems from all sources, including water, tidal, and nuclear; establishment of an REA Power Supply Division to promote adequate supply of power; promotion and protection of "cooperative territorial integrity"; and a unified attempt to secure favorable legislation on a state level for the electrical cooperative frame of reference.[26]

This present and projected loan policy goes well beyond anything contemplated by the proponents of the 1936 Act. Representative Rayburn, during the congressional debates on the REA loan function, noted:

> Now allow me to refer for a moment to another statement made by the gentleman from Connecticut [Mr. Merritt] in which he thinks we are going to socialize things by measures such as this. I do not believe in socializing this industry. I think the industry should remain in private hands and Mr. Cooke, the Administrator, believes the same thing.

And again:

> May I say to the gentleman that we are not, in that bill, intending to go out and compete with anybody. By this bill we hope to bring electrification to people who do not now have it. This bill was not written on the theory that we were going to punish somebody or parallel

---

[26] 1961 Regional Meetings of National Rural Electric Cooperative Associations in Eau Claire, Wisconsin; Columbus, Ohio; Mobile, Alabama; Richmond, Virginia; El Paso, Texas; Bismarck, North Dakota; Cheyenne, Wyoming; New Orleans, Louisiana; Sacramento, California; and Hollywood, Florida.

17

their lines or enter into competition with them. It was our thought that in the States where electricity is not generated and distributed, the laws of that State would control the rates. May I say further that the Rural Electrification Administration will have nothing whatsoever to do with the rates that may be fixed in these communities, for the simple reason that the matter will be controlled by State law.[27]

In 1961 there were comparable statements calculated to put at rest fears of further government encroachment in the electrical power industry. During hearings before the subcommittee of the House Committee on Appropriations, in the spring of 1961, Chairman Jamie L. Whitten stated:

> I do think that it is important, however, not to put the private companies out of business, but to see that they give reasonable contracts in time and in cost to their coop customers . . . I subscribe to the fact that, since the Government has to have taxes anyway you take it, the Government can't provide sound REA loans except from taxes. These taxes are obtained from private enterprise, not from Government enterprise or from the sale of bonds, which, in turn, must be predicated on tax income. So I think anybody who studies it realizes that the REA—as sound and as solid as it is—should not be used for the purpose of putting the private companies out of business.[28]

In these hearings, REA Administrator Clapp voiced substantially the same opinion: "I want to assure you and assure the Committee that at REA we do not consider our program is designed or should be used to put power companies out of business."[29]

---

[27] *Congressional Record*, 74th Congress, 2d Session, pp. 5281 and 5283.
[28] *Agricultural Appropriations for 1962, House Hearings, op. cit.*, p. 473.
[29] *Ibid.*, p. 474.

THE CHANGE IN ORIENTATION

PRIOR TO WORLD WAR II, over 80 percent of the customers of REA-borrowers lived on farms. At the present time, about 50 percent of these customers are non-farm, as are three of every four new ones. Former REA Administrator David Hamil, in the hearings on appropriations for fiscal 1961, observed that by 1965 this new orientation of REA programs would result in more non-farm than farm customers on borrowers' lines.[1]

It should be noted that there is nothing in the REA Act which explicitly restricts the program to serving farms. Neverthe-

[1] *Ibid.*, p. 492.

less, in the minds of the public, the image of REA is that of an agency whose function is to bring electricity to the farm. This image, however, is becoming more and more illusory. But as a strategem for the indefinite continuation of REA activity it evidently serves a useful purpose. REA's function may have changed, but its reports do not stress this fact. Those opposing the new direction are typically regarded by REA spokesmen as agents of the "power lobby."

From Farm to Non-Farm Customers

Section 2 of the 1936 Act authorized the REA Administrator to make loans "for rural electrification and the furnishing of electric energy to persons in rural areas who are not receiving central station service." It should be noted here that (1) the persons to be served are to be in rural areas—a term subsequently defined in the law; and (2) they must be persons not receiving central station service.

In section 13, the term "rural areas" is defined as meaning "any area of the United States not included within the boundaries of any city, village, or borough having population in excess of 1,500 inhabitants and such terms shall be deemed to include both farm and non-farm population thereof; the term 'farm' shall be deemed to mean a farm as defined in the publications of the Bureau of the Census; the term 'person' shall be deemed to mean any natural person, firm, corporation, or association." Thus, rural areas include not only unincorporated areas, but also villages, cities, or towns with a population of 1,500 or less; and they embrace non-farm as well as farm population.

The number of farms in each state without central station service was to constitute the basis for distributing among the states the loan funds available each year. Thus, Congress clearly indicated its intention that REA was to bring electricity to farms. Section 3(c) provided that 50 percent of the available funds was to be allocated yearly among the several states in the proportion which the number of their farms not then receiving central station electric service bore to the total number of such farms in the United States. The remainder was to be allocated among the states as the Administrator might see fit, but not more than 10 percent was to be loaned in any one state. In 1955 this subsection was amended so that only 25 percent might be allocated on the basis of farms not served.[2] Funds so allocated but not spent may be reallocated as the Administrator wishes, but not more than 25 percent can be spent in any one state. The remaining 75 percent can be spent as the Administrator wishes, but again not more than 25 percent can be loaned in any one state.

Thus, when the original law was enacted in 1936, although loan funds could be used in rural areas to serve both farms and non-farm customers, the method provided for allocating funds was directly tied to farms not receiving central electric service. The 1955 modification was inevitable as the proportion of farms not receiving electric service declined. And so, although the distribution of unelectrified farms now plays a smaller role in the allocation of funds, nevertheless the only formula explicitly provided in the law still is based on their number in each state. Any further revision in the formula for allocating funds is a matter for conjecture: to do so would tend to point up the ambiguity in the popular image of REA and focus attention on its new orientation.

As stated in section 2 of the law, REA-borrowers may furnish electricity to "persons in rural areas who are not receiving central station service." This sweeping generalization has placed REA in the forefront of electrification of wide areas of the U. S. during the past 25 years. At the present time, as noted, the emphasis is upon rural non-farm customers.

The record of the original congressional discussion of the bill, however, reveals no inkling of this present re-orientation. The answers of Senator Norris to questions asked by Senators McNary and King, during the debate of February 25, 1936, make clear the intent of section 2:

> MR. McNARY. I have my own idea as to the interpretation and definition of the expression "electrification of rural areas not receiving central-station electric light and power service." What interpretation does the Senator place upon that language? Could he illustrate it?

[2] Act of June 15, 1955, P.L. 70, 69 Stat. 131.

MR. NORRIS. That means, as I understand, and as I think the present administration is now doing, that there will not be set up an organization and money loaned to it for the purpose of electrifying a rural area which is now supplied. There are now, of course, a large number of rural districts already supplied with electricity from central power stations. But it does not mean that the agency proposed to be established will be prohibited from going into a locality where there may be a large number of local plants used by individual farmers. In a great many places generators of various kinds produce electricity locally for some particular farmers. The language referred to would not prohibit the setting up of an organization in a locality where that kind of supply was already in existence.[3]

From this statement it might be inferred that Senator Norris did not contemplate that REA would go into an area already served by a central station. However, he noted that where individual farms are using their own plants or a group has its own generator, REA loans would be permitted:

MR. McNARY. We probably are together generally, but under the language used, it seems to me, where a plant is now in existence which is adequately supplying a certain area none of the money provided by the bill could be used for that purpose.

MR. NORRIS. That is as I understand it.

MR. McNARY. I agree with that, but supposing that some central station by the construction of distribution lines and transmission lines could supply the energy needed in a given area, could the money be used for that purpose?

MR. NORRIS. If I understand the Senator's question correctly, it is supposing some locality be now supplied from a central station, might it be possible for that central station to extend its lines further and would the governmental agency be prohibited from entering that territory? If that is the question, I think not.

MR. McNARY. I think we want a definite meaning fixed, because I think it is an important proposition. The prohibition would relate to a central station furnishing light and power in an area that is now enjoying adequate service. Is that the Senator's interpretation?

MR. NORRIS. Yes.[4]

Senator King questioned Senator Norris is similar vein:

MR. KING. Assume that an area which is now covered by the power plant in Washington extends into Virginia, say, 10 miles beyond the District line—and I am using this as an illustration without knowing anything about the facts—and adequate lighting facilities are furnished to all farmers within that area who desire such facilities, and

---

[3] *Congressional Record*, 74th Congress, 2d Session, p. 2751.
[4] *Ibid.*

suppose a corporation is organized under the law of Maryland to furnish light to farmers a little beyond the area where the lighting is now furnished; would that corporation when organized be permitted to come within the 10 mile area to which I have referred and enter into competition with the company now furnishing light there?

MR. NORRIS. The Senator says "come into competition." They would not come in competition with farms already supplied. They might come in competition with the central power company.

MR. KING. That is not my question.

MR. NORRIS. There is no intention of going into a farming community which is already supplied with electric current and forming farm organizations there and having them built up to go into competition, as the Senator suggests, with farmers who are already getting their electric from a central station.

MR. KING. If an organization were formed beyond the 10-mile limit to which I have just referred and within which limit the farmers are supplied with electric energy, that organization would not be permitted to come back into the 10-mile area to furnish light to farmers already receiving it?

MR. NORRIS. Not to those already receiving it, but it might come into the 10-mile area and supply farmers who were not receiving it. That is the distinction which I think ought to be drawn.[5]

The Decline of the Farm Sector

Both the number of farms and the total farm population have declined significantly since 1936. In 1936 there were 6,640,000 farms in the United States; in 1959 there were 3,704,000, a decline of approximately 44 percent. Table IV indicates this decline over the last three decades.

Table IV
TOTAL FARMS IN THE UNITED STATES
FOR SELECTED YEARS

Year	No. of farms
1959	3,704,000
1954	4,782,000
1950	5,382,000
1945	5,859,000
1940	6,097,000
1936	6,640,000
1930	6,289,000

Source: *Statistical Abstract of the United States, 1962*, p. 610.

[5] *Ibid.*

With occasional exceptions, total farm population has also steadily declined—relative to total population, from 24.8 percent in 1936 to 11.4 percent in 1960.

Table V

FARM POPULATION AS A PERCENT OF TOTAL POPULATION

Year	Farm population	Percent of total population	Year	Farm population	Percent of total population
1960...........	20,541,000	11.4[1]			
1959...........	21,172,000	12.0	1948	25,903,000	17.7
1958...........	21,388,000	12.3	1947	27,124,000	18.9
1957...........	21,606,000	12.7	1946	26,286,000	18.8
1956...........	22,362,000	13.3	1945	25,295,000	18.1
1955...........	22,438,000	13.6	1944	25,495,000	18.5
1954...........	22,099,000	13.7	1943	26,681,000	19.6
1953...........	22,679,000	14.3	1942	29,234,000	21.7
1952...........	24,283,000	15.5	1941	30,273,000	22.7
1951...........	24,160,000	15.7	1938	30,980,000	23.9
1950...........	25,058,000	16.6	1936	31,737,000	24.8
1949...........	25,954,000	17.5			

[1] This figure is based on the old census definition, applicable from 1936 through 1959. According to the new definition of a "farm," adopted in 1960, the 1960 farm population would be 15,635,000 or but 8.7 percent of total population; for 1961, the total had dropped to 14,803,000, or 8.1 percent.

Source: *Statistical Abstract of the United States, 1962*, p. 608.

According to the new definition used in the 1960 census, the farm population consists of all persons living in rural territory on places of less than ten acres yielding agricultural products which sold for $250 or more in the previous year, or on places of ten acres or more yielding agricultural products which sold for $50 or more in the previous year.

Along with the decline in farm population and the number of farms has come an *increase* in realized gross income of farmers, as indicated in Table VI.

24

Table VI

REALIZED GROSS INCOME OF FARMERS

Year	Realized gross income
1961	$39,555,000,000
1960	38,068,000,000
1959	37,514,000,000
1958	37,907,000,000
1957	34,389,000,000
1955	33,332,000,000
1950	32,482,000,000
1945	25,772,000,000
1940	11,038,000,000

Source: *Statistical Abstract of the United States, 1962*, p. 630.

Table VII points up the great change in REA's emphasis from 1947 through 1961. Of about 100,000 new units served annually by REA-borrowers, three out of four are now non-farm users—both residential and industrial units. In many cases, REA service was already available and was demanded by the new units. Frequently, however, the new service involved heavying up the lines and increasing the generating facilities. There has also been the inducement of securing power at a lower cost.

The table also shows that in 1947, 76.9 percent of consumers served by REA-borrowers were farms; in 1959, only 55.2 percent were farms. It is especially pertinent to note in this connection that, starting with the year 1960, farm service is no longer reported separately but is included with "residential service farm, non-farm, and seasonal." The figure for this comprehensive group in 1961 was estimated at 84 percent. Thus, a casual reader might infer that 84 percent of the consumers were on farms. This disguises what actually is taking place: that the expansion of REA loans has accompanied industrial growth and residential development in rural areas. It will also be noted that the number of residential consumers in towns, in commercial and industrial (small), and in commercial and industrial (large) who receive service from REA-borrowers has more than doubled in the last 15 years.

Table VII

CONSUMERS SERVED BY REA-BORROWERS, 1947-61

As of	Total		Farms		Residential service Non-farm rural		Residential service Towns		Commercial and Industrial Small		Commercial and Industrial Large a		Other b	
	1,000's	%	1,000's	%	1,000's	%	1,000's	%	1,000's	%	1,000's	%	1,000's	%
1961c	4,891	100.0	d	d	4,108	84.0	343	7.0	373	7.6	15	0.3	52	1.1
1960	4,767	100.0	d	d	4,003	84.0	335	7.0	363	7.6	15	0.3	51	1.1
1959	4,654	100.0	2,567	55.2	1,352	29.0	323	6.9	352	7.6	13	0.3	47	1.0
1958	4,522	100.0	2,541	56.2	1,281	28.3	304	6.7	339	7.5	12	0.3	45	1.0
1957	4,407	100.0	2,504	56.8	1,232e	28.0	292	6.7	327	7.4	11	0.2	41	0.9
1956	4,302	100.0	2,474	57.5	1,179e	27.4	288	6.7	318	7.4	9	0.2	34	0.8
1955	4,188	100.0	2,437	58.2	1,148	27.4	264	6.3	306	7.3	8	0.2	25	0.6
1954	4,109	100.0	2,704	65.8	846	20.6	242	5.9	288	7.0	8	0.2	21	0.5
1953	3,952	100.0	2,640	66.8	786	19.9	229	5.8	269	6.8	8	0.2	20	0.5
1952	3,769	100.0	2,540	67.4	720	19.1	219	5.8	253	6.7	7	0.2	30	0.8
1951	3,547	100.0	2,359	66.5	720	20.3	198	5.6	238	6.7	7	0.2	25	0.7
1950	3,252	100.0	2,553	78.5	280	8.6	176	5.4	218	6.7	6	0.2	19	0.6
1949	2,778	100.0	2,175	78.3	247	8.9	150	5.4	189	6.8	6	0.2	11	0.4
1948	2,264	100.0	1,745	77.1	206	9.1	138	6.1	161	7.1	7	0.3	7	0.3
1947	1,843	100.0	1,417	76.9	146	7.9	133	7.2	135	7.3	7	0.4	5	0.3

a Borrowers do not have a classification of "industrial consumers." The term "commercial and industrial" consumers as used by REA-borrowers is defined as:

Small—Generally includes establishments with installed transformer capacity of 25 kilovolt-amperes kilowatts. This category includes schools, churches, and halls.

Large—Generally includes establishments with installed transformer capacity of over 25 kilovolt-amperes. Borrowers purchasing power from TVA include in this class consumers with a demand of 50 kilowatts and over.

b Includes pump irrigation, public street and highway lighting, and other electric service.

c Preliminary.

d Farm service is no longer reported separately beginning with 1960. The category for 1960 and future years is residential service including farm, non-farm, and seasonal.

e Includes seasonal cottages.

Source: Hearings before the subcommittee of the Senate Committee on Appropriations, *Agricultural Appropriations for 1959*, p. 65. Information for years 1958-61 was secured from the Rural Electrification Administration, February 5, 1962.

Growth of the Non-Farm Sector

Postwar population growth has transformed many sections of rural America into evergrowing power markets with steadily mounting demand. This situation intensifies the possibility of conflict between private power companies and rural electrical cooperatives. When REA was established, the terms "rural areas" and "farms" were used interchangeably. But with the non-farm population movement into rural areas, there is an evident need to make a new distinction in this terminology—and, more basically, in REA's frame of reference.

Metropolitan Expansion. In 1950, the Bureau of the Census recognized 172 standard metropolitan areas within the United States, Hawaii, and Puerto Rico. As of June 1960, it recognized 212 such areas—central cities of 50,000 or more population along with their contiguous suburban areas. Eighty-four percent of the increase in the nation's population during the 1950-60 decade occurred in the metropolitan areas, and of this growth, 80 percent took place in the suburbs and fringe areas. A population projection by the Census Bureau is for a population of 220 million by 1975, with 80 million living in the expanding suburbs and fringes of metropolitan districts.[6]

As metropolitan areas expand into the countryside, what were once rural areas become urbanized. At the present time, vacant land of the fringe areas is being absorbed into metropolitan complexes at the rate of about one million acres per year. The new metropolitan area boundaries are difficult to place. They ignore old geographical boundaries, the political lines of districts, villages, towns, cities, counties, and states. From 1948 to 1960 the number of cities annexing rural areas more than tripled, and the number of square miles annexed increased nearly four times. In 1960, 712 cities with populations of at least 5,000 annexed more than 1,000 square miles of what had once been rural areas.[7]

---

[6] 87th Congress, 1st Session, Report by the Advisory Commission on Intergovernmental Relations, *Governmental Structure, Organization and Planning Metropolitan Areas*, 1961, pp. 5-6.

[7] Norman M. Clapp, "Crisis in Rural Electrification," Remarks Before 1961 Regional Meetings of National Rural Electric Cooperative Association, p. 5.

Homebuilding and industrial plant construction are in the forefront of this outward push; retail trades, household services, warehousing and other industrial services are rapidly adapting themselves to the new locations. Eleven million of the 13 million dwelling units erected in non-farm areas between 1946 and 1958 were located outside of central cities. Technological advances, especially in the field of transportation, have made possible this tremendous dispersion of homes, shops, and plants.[8]

The Morgan County Cooperative. The Morgan County Rural Electric Cooperative, Martinsville, Indiana, represents a typical case history of the growth of a cooperative located near an urban center. Allocated an area near Indianapolis by the Indiana Public Service Commission, it was incorporated in June 1939 to bring electricity to farms. It began serving customers in September 1940, and by 1954 service had been made available to all farms and rural residents within its allotted area.

The manager of this co-op, testifying in 1958 as to the reorientation of the co-op's purposes, stated that a new type of customer was by then applying for electric service. Ninety-five percent of new members were urban dwellers rather than farmers. In 1940, by contrast, only one of five new members had been non-farm. He concluded by noting:

> It will be necessary that the Morgan County REMC and other electrical cooperatives in like areas of this country, be able to receive low-cost loans for some time to come if they are able to carry out the long-range electrification program they have started, and have obligated themselves to do. However, the feasibility of repaying the Federal Government the funds we have borrowed will be increased greatly if we can continue to serve these new members that are applying for service.[9]

Table VIII clearly indicates the change in the customers served.

---

[8] Committee for Economic Development, *Guiding Metropolitan Growth* (Washington, 1960), p. 17.

[9] 85th Congress, 2d Session, House Committee on Government Operations, *Hearings on the Reorganization of Rural Electrification Administration*, pp. 69-70.

Table VIII

TREND OF FARM AND NON-FARM MEMBERS SERVED BY THE
MORGAN COUNTY RURAL MEMBERSHIP COOPERATIVES

	Total members	Farm members		Non-farm members	
		Number	Percent	Number	Percent
1962 (estimate)	9,800	3,250	33	6,550	67
1957	8,150	3,200	39	4,950	61
1956	7,840	3,180	41	4,660	59
1955	7,410	3,160	43	4,250	57
1954	6,970	3,130	45	3,810	55
1953	6,400	3,090	48	3,310	52
1952	5,780	3,050	53	2,730	47
1951	5,370	3,000	56	2,370	44
1950	4,980	2,950	59	2,030	41
1949	4,570	2,900	63	1,670	37
1948	4,130	2,800	68	1,330	32
1947	2,640	1,980	75	660	25

Source: 85th Congress, 2d Session, House Committee on Government Operations, *Hearings on Reorganization of Rural Electrification Administration*, p. 72.

Service in Non-Rural Areas

As Table VII shows, an increasingly large number of non-farm consumers are being served by REA-borrowers. Although the Act states that REA loans may be made only to serve persons in rural areas, there are several circumstances under which REA-borrowers' facilities may be used to provide service to persons in non-rural areas. Not only is the "farm" criterion of REA's function increasingly illusory; even the distinction between "rural" and "non-rural" has become blurred.

An Increase in Population. Should a town or village increase in population to more than 1,500 after service begins, the REA-borrower does not necessarily have to stop serving the community, nor must it cease to take on new customers. REA philosophy has been that it may even make new loans to provide facilities to meet the expanding power needs of such a community. "It is clear that so far as the Act is concerned, such a borrower may continue to provide service and REA may continue to make loans for system improvements or connections to the system, since the character of the area for purposes of the 'rural area' definition is determined as of the time the initial loan for a system is made." [10] Thus, once an area is defined as "rural" (under the 1936 Act), it remains "rural"—time, growth, and changing circumstances notwithstanding. In 1955, REA-borrowers served at least 52,018 customers in 74 towns which grew to more than 1,500 population after the initial loan was approved.[11]

Municipal Annexation. Loans have been made to borrowers for construction of facilities to serve persons in an area rural at the time of the loan but subsequently annexed by a municipality with a population in excess of 1,500. REA continues to regard this system, too, as one for which it may loan money— on the same grounds as above. As of April 1959, based on borrowers reports, 103 borrowers served 30,279 consumers in 143 towns within this category.[12]

Acquisition. REA has made loans for the acquisition of existing power facilities even where those facilities serve places with more than 1,500 residents. Loans have been approved for acquisition of facilities serving some such towns even in the face of numerous legal obstacles. The law states that loans may be made for the construction of distribution systems as well as generating and transmission facilities, and the term "construction" has been interpreted to cover not merely the actual construction of lines but also the acquisition by purchase of existing systems. The purchase of such facilities is regarded as an incidental and necessary method of bringing service to unserved persons in rural areas (Comptroller General's Opinion No. B-29463, December 1, 1942).[13]

The Solicitor of the Department of Agriculture has construed the term "construction" to cover also the *formation* of a distribution system; hence, such formation can be achieved through

[10] 86th Congress, subcommittee of the Senate Committee on Appropriations, *Supplement to Hearings on Agricultural Appropriations for 1960*, p. 5. This statement represents the official view of REA as expressed by K. L. Scott, director, Agricultural Credit Services.

[11] *Ibid.*, p. 7.

[12] *Ibid.*, p. 6.

[13] *Ibid.*, p. 5.

purchase. Such loans must provide for new services in rural areas, to be sure, because the explicit purpose is to bring service to rural areas. Thus, in all cases there must be a reasonable finding that the acquisition of the existing services will contribute substantially to the rendering of services to a significant number of unserved persons in rural areas. Persons not residing in rural areas can be served by an acquired facility if serving them is incidental to serving rural areas. The general criterion is that the entire system of the borrower must be *predominantly* rural in nature. In 1959, 54 REA-borrowers served 50,599 consumers in 78 towns with a population exceeding 1,500 even at the time such service began.[14]

Non-REA Loan Funds. In this situation, REA-borrowers have not used REA loan funds but rather their own general funds (operating revenues and other non-REA loan funds) for construction of facilities to serve customers in towns of over 1,500 population. In addition, there are cases where the necessary construction has been provided by the consumer of the electricity. There have been other cases where REA-borrowers secured loans from TVA to finance construction and then refinanced such indebtedness with an REA loan.[15]

An interesting aspect of this information about users located in non-rural areas is that the data were not available either in REA records or in those of the National Rural Electric Cooperative Association until requested by the Senate subcommittee handling appropriations for the Department of Agriculture and related agencies. On March 20, 1959, REA Administrator David A. Hamil contacted all REA electric borrowers for this data. With the changing orientation of REA lending to non-farm users, it seems obvious that this information must be kept current if REA's present policy is to be rationally evaluated.

The Legal Aspect

The legality of REA loans to borrowers serving consumers in these four non-farm categories has been established over the years in the opinions of solicitors and general counsels of the

---

[14] *Ibid.,* pp. 5-6.
[15] *Ibid.,* p. 5.

Department of Agriculture. When a cooperative and a power company serve consumers within the corporate limits of a municipality having a population in excess of 1,500, jurisdictional and territorial problems may well arise. First, there may be the need for a municipal franchise; and secondly, in its statute of incorporation, the cooperative does not have the corporate power to operate within the confines of a non-rural area such as a municipality.[16]

The Franchise. There have been a number of cases involving franchises. Generally speaking, court decisions have taken the position that facilities once lawfully installed may not be interfered with by a municipality which may annex the area in which such facilities are located. Courts have ruled that such action would result in an impairment of contract, in violation of article I of the Constitution.

A key case is *Russell* v. *Sebastian*, 233 U.S. 195 (1914), where under a state constitutional provision, a water company laid pipe. Later the state provision was amended to require the consent of the municipality. The United States Supreme Court held that such action impaired a contract and noted that:

> Moreover, the [state constitutional] provision plainly contemplated the establishment of a plant devoted to the described public service and an assumption of the duty to perform that service. That the grant, resulting from the state's offer, constituted a contract, and vested in the accepting individual or corporation a property right, protected by the Federal Constitution, is not open to dispute in view of the repeated decisions of this court. . . .

In *Town of Gans* v. *Cookson Hills Electric Cooperative*, 288 P. 2d 707 (Okla., 1955), the town incorporated and then suit was brought to expel the cooperative facilities from the town. The court in this case held that the cooperative could not be compelled to remove its facilities but did limit its operations to those facilities as of the time of incorporation and specified that further construction or operation of additional facilities be governed by town franchise.

---

[16] U. S. Department of Agriculture, Office of the General Counsel, *Legal Aspects of Territorial Protection for REA Financed Cooperatives*, January 1961. The memorandum condenses and makes current a series of memoranda and supplements prepared by the office of the General Counsel at various times, beginning January 1957.

On the other hand, in *Nolin RECC* v. *Public Service Commission et al.,* No. 57812, Cir. Ct. Franklin County, Ky., April 15, 1960, the court upheld the cooperative's right to remain and extend new service in an area incorporated into the city of Elizabethtown:

> It is also true, as the Appellants [the Cooperative] argued, that if cooperatives which properly occupy territory later annexed by a municipality cannot keep it, then the feasibility of their loans from the Rural Electrification Administration could be seriously jeopardized. The Federal Government could only loan money to construct rural electric lines at its peril that those lines might some day be made worthless by annexation. I do not believe that this is the intent of the law, Federal or State.

In the case of the *Duke Power Company and Town of Hudson* v. *Blue Ridge Electric Corporation,* No. 311, N.C. Sup. Ct. Jan. 1961, the court held that no franchise was required from the town because the town's franchise power was qualified by the authority given the North Carolina Rural Electrification Authority in approving cooperative charters.

Corporate Power to Operate. Most frequently the legal problem is a dual one, i.e., that of the franchise and the corporate power company. Thus, the cooperative charter in some states may specifically state that the purpose of the cooperative is to furnish service to persons in rural areas. The problem of operating in a non-rural area arises when subsequent annexation or incorporation of the area occurs.

Court cases have been about equally divided as to the right of the cooperative to operate in the non-rural areas. Court decisions which permit the cooperatives to remain have not held, however, that the cooperative may extend its service in the non-rural area to consumers not served prior to the annexation or incorporation of the area.

In the case of *Farmers Electric Cooperative Corporation* v. *Arkansas Power & Light Company,* 220 Ark. 652, 249 S.W. 2d 837 (1952), the court held that the cooperative in the rural area annexed by the city of Newport had no right to operate and was required to remove its facilities as the cooperative members were no longer eligible for membership.

33

An opposing decision was reached in the case of *State* v. *Upshur Rural Electric Cooperative Corporation,* 298, S. W. 2d 805 (Tex., 1957) where it was held that the cooperative could continue to provide service in the area in question but was not to extend service to persons not cooperative members prior to annexation:

> Lawful membership, once acquired, is not terminated by annexation by a city of the area in which the member resides. . . . Since members retain that status after annexation and hence the Cooperative is expressly authorized to supply electric energy to its members, it is our view that it is authorized to continue that service to them after annexation.

In the case of *City of Moultrie* v. *Colquitt County Rural Electric Company,* 211 Georgia 842, 89 S.E. 2d 657 (1955), where the cooperative had received applications for service from consumers several days after annexation into the city of Moultrie, the cooperative was not permitted to serve the applicants because of the rural area limitation.

As early as 1939, the Comptroller General in the city of Black River Falls opinion (No. B-651) ruled that a loan need not be invalidated by the fact that beneficiaries might fall outside the explicit purpose of the loan. In this case, the city of Black River Falls, with a population of about 2,000 and owning its own hydroelectric system, entered into an agreement with an REA-borrower for an interchange of energy so that at certain times of the year the borrower would sell energy to the city and, at other times, would purchase energy from the city. The interchange agreement was held to be an exercise of an incidental power: i.e., the essential purpose of the loan was not that of furnishing electric energy to residents of Black River Falls. The Comptroller General's ruling on this case noted that:

> On the basis of the statement of facts as presented in your letter, there appears ample justification for the conclusion that the primary purpose of the proposed increase in the amount of the loan and the interchange agreement is the furnishing of electric energy to persons in rural areas as provided for under the statute. Therefore, I have to advise that if the proposed loan is otherwise legal and proper, the fact that, as a result of the interchange agreement, a city having a population in excess of 1,500 inhabitants may derive some benefit as an incident of the loan does not require that the proposed increase in the loan be regarded as beyond the scope of the authority vested in the Administration under the applicable statute.

Loans for Industrial Purposes

Section 5 of the 1936 Act, as amended, authorizes the Administrator "to make loans for the purpose of financing the wiring of the premises of persons in rural areas and the acquisition and installation of electrical and plumbing appliances and equipment." Section 13 of the Act defines the term "person" to mean "any natural person, firm, corporation, or association. . . ." Therefore, under the language of the Act, an industrial enterprise can be the legal recipient of such a loan.

However, there was no question at the time the Act was passed that section 5 loans were intended to promote the use of electricity for farm and rural dwellings. Senator Norris, one of the sponsors of the bill, made this clear during the Senate debate on the REA Act:

> This reminds me to say to the Senator that the lending of money for the wiring of houses and the purchase of electrical appliances is nearly as necessary as the lending of money for the construction of lines. The construction of the lines, enabling electricity to reach a community, will be of no value whatever unless those who are to use electric lines have electrical appliances suitable for the consumption of electricity.[17]

Until recently, policy and procedure governing section 5 loans permitted them to finance for "farm steads and rural residences" the purchase and installation of wiring or rewiring, light fixtures, water pumps, plumbing and plumbing appliances and equipment, electrical household appliances, electric farm equipment, heat pumps, and other electrical house heating and air-conditioning units, and electrically-driven irrigation pumps and associated wiring and control equipment.

On July 11, 1961, REA policy was revised and the language limiting financing to "farm steads and rural residences" was eliminated; a new category was added which provided for the financing, purchase, and installation of electrical machinery and equipment for agricultural, commercial, *and industrial enterprises.*

On September 8, 1961, REA announced its first section 5 "rural areas development" loan in the amount of $25,000. This

---

[17] *Congressional Record,* 74th Congress, 2d Session, p. 2820.

loan was granted to a North Dakota electric cooperative for relending to Thompson Construction, Inc. of Velva, North Dakota, to purchase and install electrically-powered gravel crushing and washing machinery.

On October 11, 1961, REA made its second such loan, in the amount of $280,000, to the Roseau Electric Cooperative of Warrod, Minnesota. This was reloaned by the cooperative to two grain and seed processing firms, for the installation of new electrical equipment and machinery.

On December 28, 1961, REA issued a third loan, this time $30,000 to the Jo-Carroll Electric Cooperative, Elisabeth, Illinois. These funds were to be reloaned to the Chestnut Hills Resort, Inc. of Hanover, Illinois, to help purchase and install electrically-powered snow-making equipment and outdoor lights. The purpose of the snow-making equipment was to increase the number of skiing days per season and improve the quality of the ski slopes owned by this company. The outdoor lights were for illuminating the area for night skiing.

An informal account of the Illinois loan was given in the *Wall Street Journal,* April 6, 1962—unofficial but surely revealing:

> For a first hand look at the fruits of one such loan, saunter into the 96 foot-long cedar lodge of Chestnut Hills Resort, perched on a hilltop near Hanover, Illinois, 170 miles northwest of Chicago. The resort, just ending its first full winter of operation, borrowed some $30,000 through the local REA co-op to acquire two electrical compressors for snow-making equipment, eight motors to drive rope tows and provide lights for night skiing.

> Kenneth Hansen, 33, and his partner, Ronald Jirik, 32, former Chicago contractors, have an investment of $550,000 in the rolling 228-acre site and the two-level lodge, which includes four fireplaces, a 42-foot bar, a cafeteria and a dance floor. Equipment includes eight rope tows and a chair lift to hoist skiers back up the slopes. The two owners owe roughly $220,000 to bankers, finance companies and individuals, all of it in short-term loans of under two years' maturity at interest rates as high as 15%. The $30,000 REA loan, by contrast, is at 4% and is to be repaid quarterly over a ten-year period.

> *A Big Fat Loss.* The resort grossed $32,544 in 1961, but operated only two weekends in the winter of 1960-61, using three rope tows and no snow-making equipment. With the limited facilities "the first year produced a big fat loss," reflects Mr. Hansen sadly.

"We couldn't borrow more money anywhere, although we were offering to pay 18% interest," reflects Mr. Hansen, a lean, blond man raised in Norway. But then the entrepreneurs learned that, as customers of the local REA co-op, they were eligible for Government money if they would use it to build the co-op's power sales.

"We had already ordered the snow-making equipment before we applied for the REA loan because we had to have it to operate. But, frankly, we didn't know how we were going to pay for it," Mr. Hansen notes. "The REA loan will help but it looks as if we'll have to sell stock in the firm to get out of the hole."

The rural co-op, which supplied the loan mainly to expand its own business, is profiting, however. "We figure Chestnut Hills will use roughly a million kilowatts of power this year," says Charles Youtzy, the husky, crew-cut manager of the co-op; "it would take a lot of farmers to account for that much." In 1961, the co-op sold 14 million kilowatts to 2,000 members.

The co-op is loaning the $30,000 to the resort at 4% but borrowed it it from the Treasury at 2%. Mr. Youtzy figures paperwork and other expenses of the loan will offset the 2% differential.

Since September 1961, there have been 14 such section 5 loans, totaling over $1.2 million. Senator Dominick, in a recent critique of new departures in REA loan policy, pointed out that section 5 money "is being loaned to rural co-ops at 2 percent to be repaid over 35 years, and the co-ops in turn have been lending this same money to their industrial and commercial consumers at 4 to 6 percent to be repaid over a period of 5 to 10 years. Thus, the REA has enabled its co-ops to go into the money-lending business with 2 percent money. The co-op gets its money back at 4 to 6 percent over a short term and pockets the difference." The Senator concluded that "such practices as these can seriously jeopardize the REA program and can hinder the accomplishment of its stated objectives. It was never contemplated that these co-ops were to be put into the money lending business and subsidized by the Government."[18] The House Appropriations Committee, considering REA's 1964 budget, has also leveled criticism at section 5 loans and has recommended stricter controls:

It is the opinion of the majority . . . that Congress in providing for section 5 loans intended also that they should not be made where local private business can meet the need or where it is determined that the local borrowers will provide unnecessary competition. The Administrator should also certify to the Secretary [of Agriculture] as to the necessity for section 5 loans.[19]

[18] *Congressional Record*, July 10, 1963, pp. 11676-77.
[19] 88th Congress, 1st Session, House Report No. 355, p. 8.

REA'S PROMOTIONAL ACTIVITIES

Total Area Coverage

REA HAS HELD, almost from its inception and without explicit legal basis, that everyone in an area served by a borrowing cooperative should receive electric service regardless of the cost and difficulty of extending a line to his establishment. In a letter dated March 14, 1936, to the chairman of the House Committee on Interstate and Foreign Commerce, REA Administrator Morris L. Cooke wrote:

> The only effective way to electrify rural America is to construct within each rural area a network of lines to serve every possible

customer. The policy of the utility companies has been to skim off the cream of the business. Such a policy has precluded the extension of service to nearly 90 per cent of American farms and has been paralyzing in its effect.

In areas where an REA project is contemplated, we have insisted upon the inclusion of all territory which can be covered in a self-liquidating project. This policy involves the economies of mass construction, averages the poor with the better territory, and avoids the stranding of considerable areas which cannot be self-sustaining under present conditions. Unsocial practices must give way to the policy of considering the electrification of an entire area at one time. . . . [1]

In REA's Annual Report for 1938, the social responsibilities of the program were stressed along with the need for "comprehensive development."[2] The Annual Report for 1939 called for "area development," because of the economies of large-scale construction and subsequent low rates in the sale of electricity.[3]

From the cooperatives' standpoint, the Pace Act of 1944 made "area coverage" more practical by stretching out the loan repayment period and, at the same time, reducing the interest cost to the cooperatives to 2 percent. Encouraged by the Pace Act, the area coverage concept was spelled out in the Annual Report for 1946:

> Under the area coverage plan, an REA co-op must take four definite steps: (1) It determines just what area it will serve eventually; (2) It spots on a map the location of every farm, store, school, rural home, small industry, power line, and other pertinent features within the established boundaries, and prepares load estimates of the area; (3) Its engineer designs a power system to provide service for every establishment on the map; and (4) It arranges to have the system constructed, usually a section at a time, in accordance with the engineer's plan.[4]

Again in April 1961, Administrator Clapp went clearly on record: "I can assure the Committee that we are planning to press the area coverage policy adopted by Congress vigorously in both the electric and the telephone industry."[5]

---

[1] 86th Congress, 1st Session, subcommittee of House Committee on Appropriations, *Hearings on Department of Agriculture Appropriations for 1960*, p. 1670.

[2] *Annual Report of the REA for 1938*, p. 67.

[3] *Annual Report of the REA for 1939*, p. 74.

[4] *Annual Report of the REA for 1946*, p. 22.

[5] *Agricultural Appropriations for 1962, House Hearings, op. cit.*, p. 454.

Area coverage has been a useful slogan for REA. It has served to justify large and continuing appropriations, lengthy pay-back periods, low interest rates, and extension of the co-operatives into ventures quite foreign to the initial objectives of farm electrification and rural relief.

Adoption of area coverage as an operating policy at the co-op level has not been unopposed. Thus, in 1949, REA Administrator Wickard testified:

> Yes, sir, we are having some troubles along that line, Mr. Chairman. I think we are making some progress. We have talked about area coverage for a great many years and think it has become better accepted than it was formerly. . . . There are a few instances, I suspect, where the board of directors and present members do not just see the necessity or obligations they have of extending lines out into thinner territories because they have begun to pay off their indebtedness, and they feel if they have to get out into the thinner territories, there is a danger that the time will be delayed when they are completely paid out on their indebtedness to the Government.[6]

Those "few instances" of which Administrator Wickard spoke in 1949 led to the insertion of the following provision in distribution loan contracts in January 1950:

> The Borrower shall make diligent effort to extend electric service to all unserved persons who are located within the service area of the Borrower, as such area shall from time to time be determined by the Administrator. At such time or times as the Administrator may require, the Borrower shall make diligent effort to obtain applications for membership in the Borrower or subscriptions to its capital stock, as the case may be, from all such persons, and shall accept such applications or subscriptions by appropriate corporate action.[7]

Again in 1958, this same local opposition led to the issuance of a policy statement that loan contracts should contain "appropriate provisions" to further the policy of area coverage.[8] At the present time area coverage is pointed, inevitably, toward the non-farm segment of the population.

With all this stress on area coverage, and with continuing inclusion in loan contracts of admonitions to extend service to all inhabitants of the area, there is good reason to assume that,

---

[6] 81st Congress, House Committee on Appropriations, *Hearings on Agriculture Appropriations Bill for 1950*, p. 676.
[7] *Annual Report of the REA for 1950*, p. 8.
[8] REA Bulletin 112-3, September 23, 1958.

at the operating level, many co-ops are following the practical policy of extending service to those best able to pay for it. They have evidently fallen into the habit—the burden of Administrator Cooke's 1936 charge against private power companies—of "skimming the cream" in their service areas.

Industrialization

Along with its advocacy of comprehensive area coverage, REA has also campaigned to line up industrial and commercial customers for REA-borrowers. By December 1940, 5,365 industrial establishments were buying service from REA-financed facilities. These included defense industrial units, processors of raw material, CCC camps, NYA youth-training centers, Army, Navy and Coast Guard camps, as well as other governmental services. By early 1941, Camps Shelby, Leonard Wood and Fort Salisbury were being served by REA-borrowers. A loan of over $3.6 million permitted a cooperative to serve Marine bases in North Carolina.[9]

During the war years there was a steady increase in applications received by REA-borrowers for industrial and commercial power service. Many of these came from manufacturing and processing industries—especially from plants using rural and farm products.[10]

The postwar years brought an intensification of efforts to secure commercial and industrial users. In 1958, the general manager of the Eastern Iowa Light and Power Cooperative testified as to the desirability of serving industrial consumers during off-peak hours—in order to justify a peak-load capacity representing fully 35 percent of the co-op's investment, but in use only 45 minutes each day:

> We of the Iowa rural electric cooperatives, now serving 136,000 consumers who could find no other source of electric power, feel that we have an obligation to serve rural industries located within our service area and along our existing lines.
>
> . . . We have an obligation to the rest of our members to increase the off-peak consumption of electricity in order to justify the investments

[9] *Report of the Administrator of the REA for 1941*, pp. 2-12.
[10] *Report of the Administrator of the REA for 1945*, p. 9.

we have made for maintaining quality service over the peak demands. Industrial loads will help us to do this, since the average industry on an 8-hour day will not increase our peak demand appreciably. . . .

In conclusion, gentlemen, I would like to impress upon you that this problem of who shall serve industry which chooses rural sites has occurred and will occur more and more frequently as our economy requires expansion, relocation, and dispersion of industry.[11]

REA Administrator David Hamil, in a policy statement before the NRECA convention in March 1957, stated:

Since agriculture is changing, since the very character of the countryside is changing, the cooperative is called on to change to a much broader concept of power use promotion. The rural electrification program was founded on the principle of area coverage. If we carry that principle one step further, we assume responsibility for area development.

I would like to see all of you working to attract more industry to your area, either as a part of your power use program or in cooperation with other local groups. . . . If there is any question whether you should serve industrial loads, let me say that I believe you have an obligation, both under the Rural Electrification Act and the area coverage principle, to see to it that all potential consumers are served.[12]

In 1958, Administrator Hamil restated his belief in rural industrialization with REA help. He again urged the rural cooperatives to aid the trend toward rural industrialization, mentioned with pride that non-farm consumers on the system used more power than farm consumers, and stated that three non-farm consumers were being added for each additional farm hook-up. He also said:

More and more the money which rural electric systems borrow from REA will be used to supply electricity for non-farm homes, for rural businesses, small industries and processing plants which expect to pay the going rate.[13]

An REA Bulletin issued in 1958 stated that REA is to "encourage the furtherance of balanced rural development pro-

---

[11] 85th Congress, subcommittee of the House Committee on Government Operations, *Hearings on H.R. 11762, A Bill to Amend Reorganization Plan Number 2 of 1953*, pp. 45-46.

[12] "Public Acceptance—Our Best Insurance," Statement before the subcommittee of the Senate Committee on Appropriations, *Hearings on Agricultural Appropriations for 1958*, pp. 436-39.

[13] Speech reprinted in 86th Congress, Committee on Agriculture, *Hearings on Agriculture Credit and Rural Electrification Administration Review*, February 5 and 18, 1959, pp. 68-69.

grams through better farming and industrial expansion to provide increased off-farm employment opportunities and improved education, health and welfare facilities."[14]

During the 1958 appropriations hearings, a committee member noted that, "I did not know it was the function of the REA to attract industry. I thought it was a rural electrification cooperative program." Part of the response to this observation was the following:

> Industry in rural areas provides additional income to the communities and helps to smooth out the income irregularities inherent in farming. Opportunity for off-farm employment and employment of young people has a tendency to stabilize the population of rural areas, and thereby helps with one of the more serious problems in agriculture in recent years.

> The Department of Agriculture is vigorously moving forward with its rural development program which is designed to promote balanced economic growth in rural areas. This program is expected to bring significant benefits to farm families such as better farming and homemaking; opportunities to earn income off the farm, and training to take advantage of such opportunities; improved opportunities for education; improved health and family welfare; and greater participation in community life. These are long-term goals. The attraction and development of rural industries is important to the success of this program and it is possible only if electric power for these industries is made available to them.[15]

This "vigorous" initiative has been, since 1961, the official REA line—judging from Administrator Clapp's testimony on congressional appropriations in April 1961,[16] and from Bulletin 800-1, issued July 17, 1961, dealing with rural area development. REA, through a Rural Area Development staff, will provide leadership and direct and coordinate REA rural area development; maintain liaison with other federal agencies on development; evolve its own development policies and procedures; make available specialized assistance to borrowers and their associations on rural development including promotion, stimulation, organization, financing, construction, and operation of rural enterprises; and encourage consumer loans for financing electrical equipment for commercial and industrial enterprises.[17]

---

[14] REA Bulletin 140-4, July 11, 1958.
[15] *Agricultural Appropriations for 1958, Senate Hearings, op. cit.,* p. 435.
[16] *Agricultural Appropriations for 1962, House Hearings, op. cit.,* p. 491.
[17] REA Bulletin 800-1, July 17, 1961.

Thus, as the process of bringing electricity to the farm approaches completion, REA-borrowers—openly led by REA officials—have intensified their efforts to expand the rural electrification program into other segments of the economy. Explicit policy now calls for stimulating the development of rural industry and for leadership by REA-borrowers in aiding local development corporations to promote new enterprises. REA is actively seeking new power markets—specifically within the rural non-farm sector, which grows larger each year and becomes increasingly industrialized.

Economic Implications of Non-Farm Service

In a time of general prosperity and the migration of large numbers of people to what were once rural areas, it would seem that electric power should be priced at no less than its full cost, and that this should include taxes comparable to those paid by private utilities and interest sufficient to reimburse the Federal Government for its own borrowing costs. It seems only reasonable to expect that the costs of "beefing up" a distribution system should be borne by those receiving its benefits. All the more so, when we consider that the move to suburbia from the central cities is by the moderately well-to-do—not generally by the impoverished. Transfers of the affluent from the rolls of the private utilities—which are tax-collectors—to those of the co-operatives—by and large, tax consumers—simply shifts the burden of taxes more and more upon the shoulders of the city residents and commercial establishments. It is not unreasonable to predict an acceleration of "urban blight" should this trend continue.

With every such migration from a private utility to a co-operative service area, the Federal Government is a double loser. First, it lends more and more through REA, at less than cost; and second, it loses the tax receipts formerly collected from the customer by the private company.

The cooperative movement has led nearly three decades of sheltered life. It will never become self-supporting, willing and able to pay its own way, until access to tax revenues is sharply curtailed, and until it is required to pay local, state, and federal taxes proportionate to those paid by other businesses and consumers.

Does this imply that rural citizens should be denied electricity? Not at all. Those who are able to pay should be expected to pay the full cost of the services that they demand—neither more nor less. Those who are unable to pay may continue to be supported, in part, from general tax receipts. REA's initial purpose was to make electricity available in rural areas at a price rural residents were able to pay. It chose to use the cooperative as the instrument of this purpose; but the creation of co-ops per se was never part of REA's mandate. Nor should the present emphasis on "protecting the territorial integrity" of REA-borrowers—a subject with which the next section deals—be permitted to obscure these basic facts.

With REA's active encouragement, cooperatives are now pressing for increased loans (1) to "beef up" their distribution systems to serve more non-farm residences and businesses, and (2) to acquire their own generating and transmission systems where federal power is not available in sufficient quantity to satisfy their entire needs. The cooperatives are also promoting legislation to reserve to themselves the areas they have developed. "Fair play" would suggest that, if these areas are to be fenced off as exclusive preserves, the residents of such areas should at least be required to shoulder their proportionate share of the total tax burden. Tax-free islands throughout the country are surely not consistent with the concept of "fair play," and least of all in an era of widely-shared prosperity.

GROWING EMPHASIS ON
GENERATION AND TRANSMISSION

AS WE HAVE ALREADY NOTED, the rural electrification program is in the process of major change. Vigorously encouraged by REA, more and more cooperatives have been requesting loans for construction of generation and transmission facilities. Table IX indicates the quantity and relative importance of such loans in recent years.

If the percentage of loans is indicative of the philosophy of REA, recent data clearly show that distribution of electricity to "rural areas" is of increasingly less importance than ownership of the sources of energy.

46

Table IX

GENERATING AND TRANSMISSION LOANS
APPROVED BY THE REA, 1956-62
(in thousands of dollars)

	Annual		Cumulative		KW Capacity	Total in
Year	G and T loans	% of total loans	G and T outstanding	% of total loans	Placed in service	service 6/30
1962	$149,332	58.7	$1,264,984	27.0	62,250	1,910,165
1961	151,802	55.3	1,115,769	25.1	204,937	1,847,915
1960	88,917	40.4	963,967	23.2	313,450	1,644,609
1959	64,814	36.5	885,282	22.5	140,870	1,333,611
1958	86,338	35.8	825,370	21.9	211,231	1,195,485
1957	120,144	39.9	744,832	21.0	81,078	987,778
1956	61,252	32.3	626,879	19.4	19,500	906,723

Source: Reports of the Administrator of the Rural Electrification Administration, 1956-62. Total capacity for which financing has been
provided amounted to 3,486,585 KW (net), through fiscal 1962.
Report of the Administrator, 1962, p. 4.

Further evidence comes from the testimony of Administrator
Clapp, in hearings on Department of Agriculture appropriations for 1962, in which he set forth the criteria for generation
and transmission loans:

First of all, the question is asked: Is there an adequate and dependable source of supply available to this cooperative, or these cooperatives, these borrowers? If there is not a dependable and adequate
source of supply available, then we have under our policy a reason for
extending a loan for the development of an independent source of
supply.

Secondly, has it been determined that the power available is more
expensive than the borrowers could generate and transmit if they
did it themselves? In this case, the policy is to make the loans for
these purposes.

To this we are currently adding a third criterion, and that is the
question of the future security of the borrower systems.

We have case after case come to our attention of where our distribution co-ops are attempting to negotiate contracts with the power
companies and these negotiations get bogged down over one or two
serious difficulties.

One is the question of no guarantee as to what the ceiling will be
on these power rates over a 10-year period or longer, with escalator
clauses of various kinds which clearly point to a year-by-year increase of the wholesale power rate on which these distribution systems are mainly dependent.

Then the second difficulty that is cropping up more and more frequently is the so-called dual rate in which the supplier, the commercial power company that is supplying the distribution cooperative,

says in effect: You are set up to serve farmers, and if there is any industrial load in the territory that you moved into to develop, then this is really not your load; it should be ours. If you actually do hook up these loads, then you shall pay us under our supply contract what we would have charged that consumer directly if we were supplying him directly.

With points of controversy such as these, and with rather substantial portions of some of our distribution co-ops involved in territorial disputes at this time, we at REA find that our obligation is not only to assess the question of whether or not there is actually a sufficient supply of power available at the right place and at the right time in sufficient quantity; we should not be limited to the comparative rate of generation versus purchase.[1]

Adequate and Dependable Power

The first test that an application for a generating and transmission loan must pass is that of the lack of an adequate and dependable source of supply. The overall reserve capacity in the continental United States is shown in Table X.

Table X

AVAILABLE POWER, PEAK LOAD AND RESERVE,
TOTAL ELECTRIC UTILITY INDUSTRY,
CONTINENTAL UNITED STATES, 1948-60

Year	Available power at Dec. peak load (MKW)	Non-coincident Dec. peak load (MKW)	Margin of reserve (%)
1960 (p)	174,900	133,000	31.5
1959	163,300	125,400	30.2
1958	148,600	116,900	27.1
1957	134,600	110,100	22.2
1956	126,500	105,700	19.7
1955	119,900	101,100	18.6
1954	106,500	88,400	20.4
1953	95,500	81,100	17.8
1952	84,300	75,300	11.9
1951	78,700	70,400	11.8
1950	70,900	64,300	10.3
1949	64,500	56,500	14.2
1948	57,300	53,750	6.6

(p) Preliminary.

Source: Edison Electric Institute, *Statistical Year Book of the Electric Utility Industry for 1960*, Table 5, p. 10.

[1] Hearings before the subcommittee of the House Committee on Appropriations, 87th Congress, 1st Session, pp. 4741-45.

The data indicate that an adequate supply of power is available, overall, and that the margin of reserve capacity has increased steadily. In addition, the reserve capacity in each of the eight regions of the country affords an ample margin to assure adequate and dependable supplies.[2] Some few scattered areas may be exceptions, but it is obvious that power is generally available in adequate quantities throughout the country.

Comparative Costs

The second criterion for a loan is that of the comparative cost of buying versus generating and transmission by the cooperative.

In the electric power industry, evidence abounds that economy of generation and transmission goes hand in hand with the size of the generating unit and the capacity of the transmission line. The current emphasis on G and T loans to cooperatives to build small units for self-service, shifting their sources of supply from the more efficient larger units of private industry, flies in the face of all the facts about the economics of power generation. In those jurisdictions where rates charged by the private companies are subject to approval by some public authority, the price does not exceed cost plus a fair profit. Only three conditions could explain how a cooperative might generate and transmit power at a lower cost:

1. The cooperative might install larger, more efficient units than those of its private supplier.

2. The cooperative's costs might be totaled without consideration of the cost of money to its capital supplier and without including taxes being carried by the private unit it may displace.

3. The profit allowed to the present supplier might be excessive.

As the following case illustrates, there are occasions when the first and third of these conditions seem to be unfulfilled. In a Department of Agriculture news release—date-lined Washington, June 20, 1961—it was reported that "REA approves largest electrification loan. A loan of $60,225,000 was approved to a federation of 16 REA-financed electric distribution cooperatives

---

[2] EEI, *The Investor-Owned Electric Utility Industry*, September 1961.

in southern Indiana." The loan approved for Hoosier Cooperative Energy, Inc., was for three 66,000 kilowatt steam units costing a total of $31,864,000, and for 285 miles of 154 kilovolt line
and 1,267 miles of 69 kilovolt line costing an estimated
$28,361,000. Justification advanced for approval of this loan was
that owning these facilities would "save" the customers $5.5
million in ten years. Two further facts were not stressed: (1)
that the Government would pay out in interest for the funds
reloaned at 2 percent more than this sum in ten years; and (2)
that it would lose the tax revenues from displaced private facilities.

In remarking upon the REA project, the Northern Indiana
Public Service Company (in its employee magazine, NIPSCO
Picture, No. 5, 1961) estimated that its facilities already providing this service to the cooperatives had cost $24.7 million—as
against $60 million for facilities of comparable operating effi-
ciency to do the same job.

Congressman Michel of Illinois has pointed out the great
difficulty of appraising REA loan policies:

> At the present time there seem to be no checks or balances on this
> type loan even though 40.5 per cent of last year's appropriations were
> for G and T facilities. However, the G and T loan application is held
> in absolute secrecy and it is impossible for existing suppliers to learn
> whether their wholesale business is being taken away from them or
> even given a chance to bid on a new contract which might prove
> more favorable to the farmer consumer of an REA cooperative than
> a generating plant of their own.

Congressman Michel, with reference to a letter from the president of Alabama Power Company, continued his remarks:

> This letter raised in my mind the question of what other areas
> throughout the country, including my home State of Illinois, are
> having similar problems. Therefore, I requested of the REA a list of
> G and T loan applications pending or under study similar to the list
> appearing on page 50 in the Senate Second Urgent Deficiency Ap-
> propriation Hearings of 1957. Furthermore, I thought it would be of
> interest to have these data in the Record so that all Members of
> Congress might be aware of what is being planned in their areas.
> However, I was unable to get this information put into the record of
> the hearings, even though the REA is financed by the taxpayers'
> money.[3]

---

[3] *Congressional Record*, June 6, 1961, pp. 8946-47.

The basis for approval of G and T loans has been spelled out in generalities only. The precise data upon which decisions are reached are not usually made public.

In a speech at the annual meeting of the Indiana State Chamber of Commerce (Indianapolis, December 5, 1961), Mr. Harlee Branch, Jr., president of the Southern Company, described three recent generating and transmission loans:

> . . . These loans will be used to construct electric power generating plants in the two states [Alabama and Mississippi] as well as hundreds of miles of high-voltage transmission line.
>
> The co-ops served by these two plants have historically been supplied by investor-owned and tax-paying utilities which are capable of furnishing whatever power requirements these co-ops may have in the future.
>
> At present the co-ops in Mississippi are paying our subsidiary an average of only 7.5 mills per kilowatt hour for power. It is expected that they will have to pay at least 8.5 mills for power supplied them from the REA-financed plant. Our Alabama subsidiary presently charges to co-ops in its territory an average of only 6.3 mills whereas the cooperatives have had to pay 9 mills per kilowatt hour for power obtained from an REA-financed plant already operating in that state.
>
> . . . Thus without any assured economic benefit even for the co-op customers, the taxpayers generally are being required to put up these millions [$16 million Mississippi and $20.3 million Alabama], at lower than actual interest cost, to duplicate and ultimately to render useless electric power facilities which presently carry a substantial portion of the local, state, and Federal tax loads.

The speaker charged that these loans, and the one in Indiana for over $60 million, were granted even though the private utilities to be affected were permitted neither to examine the data relied upon by REA nor to testify on them.

In the case of the Alabama loan referred to above, a Department of Agriculture release dated November 2, 1961, said approval was based on "security of the systems involved and cost of power." The release called attention to Alabama Power Company's insistence upon the right "to serve at retail whatever larger loads it chooses within the developed service areas of the cooperatives" as evidence sufficient to justify a loan to protect the security and effectiveness of the systems. And as for the cost of power, the second reason cited for approval of this loan, at no time was the cost estimate upon which the decision rested made available to the public. There was no indication that the estimated costs were calculated in terms of total cost to the public—including subsidized capital and tax-free operations— rather than that portion of cost to be assigned to the customers of these cooperatives.

Mr. E. A. Hunter of the Utah Power and Light Company, in testimony before the Senate Agriculture and Forestry Committee, February 28, 1962, called attention to REA's action on the Colorado-Ute Electric Association G and T loan. He said that members of this cooperative had been customers of his company, paying 10 to 11 mills per kilowatt-hour; that the cooperative was advised by an engineering firm that it could generate and transmit its own power at a cost of 7.5 mills; but that upon completion of its system, at a cost of $16 million instead of an estimated $10 million, its members had to pay 10 to 11.5 mills per kilowatt-hour. Despite such evidence of the reliability of estimates upon which the decision to grant the loan rested, this cooperative sought additional loans to expand its G and T facilities. Mr. Hunter continued:

> This cooperative now has its 38,000 kilowatt plant and through contracts for firm power with the Bureau of Reclamation, has sufficient capacity to last it for a number of years. Furthermore, it is situated almost next door to the Bureau's Upper Colorado River development which when completed in 1963 and 1964 will have over a million kilowatts of electric generating capacity. This cooperative is a preference customer and the Bureau of Reclamation has counted on it as a consumer for a part of the Colorado project's electric generation.
>
> Despite this situation, the Colorado-Ute Cooperative now seeks a $20 million loan to construct the first 150,000 kilowatt unit of an ultimate 600,000 kilowatt steam-electric generating plant. It admits that it has no use for such block of capacity but states that it would sell 100,000 kilowatts of capacity to the Salt River Power District, located some 750 miles to the south. The Salt River District serves a part of metropolitan Phoenix, Arizona, and the surrounding area, which has an excellent economy and certainly is not in need of a subsidy.

He might also have concluded that loans to permit co-ops to generate and transmit large blocks of power to distant metropolitan areas hardly fall within the scope of a "rural electrification" program.

Future Security

The third criterion for approval of generating and transmission loans is the future security of the borrower systems.

It should be recognized that the future security of REA-borrowers will be in jeopardy only if the cost of power is greater than the amount that they can collect from their customers or if the future power supply is uncertain. Few of the private companies supplying power to the cooperatives can be accused either of having inadequate reserve capacity at present or of failure to plan future construction sufficient to supply all anticipated demands. Thus, future security would seem to hinge on the question of the ability of the co-ops' customers to pay full cost—which, apparently, they are not now doing. Actually, the public subsidy consists of appropriations for administrative costs, the excess of cost of funds borrowed by the Federal Government over its collections from REA, and taxes foregone for customers of cooperatives. If the Government is interested in "protecting its investment"—that is to say, in protecting the pocketbooks of taxpaying citizens—the sensible procedure would seem to be to work out a program for an orderly withdrawal from REA. Instead, REA appears intent upon working out a program for an orderly increase in the Federal Government's investment in a questionable proposition. Demands upon the central tax-collector will increase at the same time that its collections decline—as taxpaying facilities are supplanted by those which are tax-exempt and tax-supported.

In a carefully balanced report—which strongly supports the continuation of REA's basic "right" to make G and T loans—the House Appropriations Committee has recently urged a tightening-up in the procedures for passing on such loan applications:

> . . . With regard to several loans it appears that satisfactory concessions or modifications might have been secured from the private suppliers if real efforts had been made. With regard to others, reasons given for granting loans do not appear too substantial. . . .
> Before public funds are loaned for power generation or transmission, a majority of the committee believes the REA Administrator . . . should make a survey, determine wherein the existing contract for power or the proposed contract is unreasonable, advise the supplier wherein such contract is unreasonable and attempt to get such

contract modified to make it reasonable. Loans should be made only when reasonable contracts cannot be obtained. . . . The Administrator should certify to the Secretary of Agriculture that each of these steps has been taken. . . .[4]

"Secrecy" of Negotiations

The REA "secrecy" policy, initiated in 1946 by the Department of Agriculture, was couched in general terms and made confidential all information in regard to loan applications—for both distribution and G and T. The rationale was that REA loans involve a banker-lender relationship, hence, are matters of privileged information. Thus, no public hearings are held on loans. No data or economic studies on which loans are based are made available to Congress, the press, the public, or interested power suppliers who are affected by the loan. On the other hand, when a privately owned utility offers securities for public sale, state and federal laws require full and complete disclosure of all factors relevant to the proposed operations.

The 1946 "secrecy" policy was confirmed in a new set of regulations issued by the Department of Agriculture in December 1961. Thus, "information received in expressed or implied confidence in connection with a contract, loan, or other benefit or service, when release of the information would impair the legitimate interests of the persons supplying the information, is regarded as 'administrative confidential.' " And this means that records so classified "shall not be subject to examination except in the performance of official duties, nor shall copies thereof be furnished upon request except in proper cases from Federal official sources or as specifically provided."[5]

A recent application by the Colorado-Ute Electric Association of Montrose, Colorado, illustrates the "secrecy" aspect of the loan process. On being asked about the loan, an REA official said: "Every detail of the loan application to REA is private and confidential, including all attachments thereto. If that's wraps . . . we are wrapping it." He noted it was not in the public interest to reveal details of the REA loan application. This information, he said, must come from the manager of Colorado-

[4] 88th Congress, 1st Session, House Report No. 355, p. 8.
[5] *Federal Register*, Vol. 26, No. 244, December 20, 1961, pp. 12155-56.

Ute—who, as it turned out, permitted some information to be revealed only after consultation with REA.[6]

In 1962, REA announced an alleged change in its policy of secrecy. A Bulletin lists the various annual, quarterly, and monthly publications which are available and notes that the agency will make information about its activities available to the public "to the maximum extent possible." [7]

The Bulletin states that after a loan is approved, REA will issue information as to the amount of the loan, its specific purpose or purposes, areas which will benefit, and the number of customers to be served. The area of greatest criticism of REA's secrecy policy has been that relating to loan application. Thus, upon receipt of a loan application, REA will henceforth make available the name and address of the applicant, date of application, amount of application, and the general purposes for which the funds are requested.

In the event, however, that the applicant wishes to withhold such information, this may be done—although subject to REA approval. This last proviso would appear, for all practical purposes, to negate any real change in REA secrecy policies. Thus, although "it is recommended that borrowers and prospective borrowers make available to the public to the maximum extent possible information about their activities," it appears that only constant congressional pressure will substantially alter this long-standing policy of secrecy in negotiations.

In this connection, it is especially interesting to note the conclusions reached by the subcommittee on Government Information (the Moss Committee) in January 1958, after a survey of agencies conducting loan activities as to the amount of public scrutiny permitted in their operations. REA was included in the inquiry. In more general terms, the subcommittee's conclusions were as follows:

> The right to know is being smothered under a blanket of Federal rules and regulations, sometimes issued with no valid basis in law. As one violation of the right to know is brought to public attention and corrected, another occurs somewhere else in the maze of Federal

---

[6] *Grand Junction Sentinel* (Colorado), December 13 and 28, 1961.

[7] REA Bulletin 20-12 (Electric), April 8, 1962.

departments and agencies which touch on every facet of American life. Federal officials appear addicted to the doctrine that they alone can decide what is best for the people to know about their own Government. This dangerous attitude has reached the point where even the Congress shall and shall not know about the operations of Federal departments and agencies. Only continued vigilance on the part of the public and the Congress can prevent Federal officials from thus chipping away one of the most important foundation stones of democratic representative government.[8]

"Backdoor Lawmaking"

Criticism of REA is mounting because its annual cost to taxpayers continues to rise, in direct proportion to the "reorientation" of its function. Congressman Bruce of Indiana made the following appraisal of REA's new emphasis on G and T loans:

> Mr. Chairman, a few minutes ago the gentleman from Illinois, a member of the Agriculture Subcommittee, referred to the addition of a third criterion to be used by REA in considering a generating and transmission loan as "backdoor lawmaking." The REA, by unilateral administrative action, has proposed to use its authority to grant such loans "to guarantee the cooperative device a permanent place in the American power industry." I believe he expressed the opinion that if REA wants to change the basic authority of its act, it should come to Congress and go through the proper procedures as do other agencies of Government. I would like to add a lusty "Amen" to the gentleman's statement. If Congress sits complacently by and allows bureaucrats to pervert the body of existing law to suit their own questionable ends, then we might as well close up shop and go home.

> But to guarantee the cooperative device a permanent place in the American power industry has nothing whatsoever to do with the specific problems of rates or service, even though the Administrator has tried to stretch it by claiming they need it to assure fair power contracts. The words of the third criterion are so broad and nebulous an REA Administrator could approve virtually any G. & T. loan under any condition irrespective of the actual need and certainly irrespective of the availability or the price of power from an alternative source.

> In other words, REA is now getting completely away from the original purpose of the act and is becoming what might be termed a rural power company. And these rural power companies will use 2-percent money and the other subsidies we are giving them to lure industry right out of your towns and cities into rural areas.

> I want to repeat there is nothing in any act of Congress that would permit REA to expand its duties as it has done in the case of the

---

[8] 85th Congress, 2d Session, House Committee on Government Operations, *Availability of Information from Federal Departments and Agencies*, p. 216.

expanding of G. & T. and section 5 loan criteria. These are not the only cases in which REA has followed this tactic, just the current ones. If REA desires to do these things; if they want to build generating plants just for the sake of building generating plants; if they want to build industries out in the rural areas just for the sake of building industries, then they should come here and get the permission of Congress and not try to do it through the back door.[9]

This comment constitutes a comprehensive summary of REA's dramatic and unauthorized evolution since 1936. At no time was authorization granted by Congress either to permit or to encourage REA-borrowers to enter into competition with existing suppliers of electricity. It was never the intent of Congress to negate prior investments by private companies, already serving rural customers at a regulated price.

With time, the pressure of groups favoring the cooperative-public power supply of electricity has caused a startling change in the philosophy of the rural electrification program. It is not today an agricultural program at all. Most customers being added to co-op lines are non-farm. The non-farm consumer is expanding his use of electricity much more rapidly than is the farm consumer. More loans are now being made for the construction of generation and transmission facilities than for distribution facilities.

Most G and T loans are being approved by REA for areas where power is abundant—without evidence to the public that costs will be reduced. G and T loans are being approved "to protect the security" of the cooperative system. But "security" is not defined, and little evidence is advanced that the cooperatives are insecure—not, at any rate, as a consequence of actions by the private power industry.

On July 24, 1963, Senators Lausche and Bennett introduced legislation which would make it clear, in section 4 of the REA Act (which authorizes G and T loans), that all such loans must have the primary purpose of furnishing "electric power and light to rural areas to which central power service is not available." Whenever this criterion is not fulfilled, "the bill would require the Rural Electrification Administration to finance its future operations in the open market." Even within this cri-

9 *Congressional Record*, June 6, 1961, pp. 8951-52.

57

terion, moreover, future REA loans would have to "bear interest at a rate equal to the average rate of interest payable by the United States of America on its marketable obligations, having maturities of 10 years or more, issued during the last preceding fiscal year in which any such obligations were issued and adjusted to the nearest one-eighth of 1 per cent." Congressman Teague (California) has introduced a companion bill in the House. Senator Lausche went on to make the following critical assessment of REA's future course:

> I believe that the Rural Electrification Administration has been an outstanding asset and a program which has brought much comfort, lightened the burdens, and stimulated the economy of our Nation's rural areas. The purpose for which the Rural Electrification Administration was created has largely been fulfilled.
>
> Its continued operations under the same terms and provisions provided in the present law permit the REA to go far beyond the original intent of the Congress and its activities now are in direct conflict to our basic free enterprise system.
>
> . . . there have been occasions when it was necessary for the Federal Government to underwrite and foster certain programs that could not be performed by private enterprise. The Rural Electrification Administration was such a program. It is only sensible, however, and in the best interests of our economy and the perpetuation of the free enterprise system that once these . . . programs have fulfilled their mission, they should be curtailed.[10]

---

[10] *Congressional Record,* July 24, 1963, pp. 12448, 12450.

ACHIEVEMENTS AND COSTS:
A BALANCE SHEET

BETWEEN 1935 AND 1960—REA's first quarter century—farms receiving central station electric service increased from 11 percent to nearly 97 percent. During the same period of time, the total number of establishments classified as farms declined by 32 percent—but their average size began to increase. And after 1940, this trend was paralleled by a steady upturn in net farm income. At present, REA-borrowers are serving more than half the nation's electrified farms.

REA also advances the argument that the example and the competition provided by its cooperative borrowers stimulated private utilities to extend service to many rural areas sooner than they otherwise would have.

REA began as one element in a general program of relief—particularly, relief of unemployment. This aspect of its purpose lasted less than a year; by 1936, REA was established as a lending agency. It became, and is justified today as, a national business investment. As such, what have been its accomplishments? What have been its costs, and to whom? What function does it now serve?

As of June 30, 1962, 1,094 REA-borrowers were operating 1,492,000 miles of line and distributing electric energy to 5,014,000 customers—with about 16 percent of this energy generated as a result of G and T loans. More than half the nation's farms are served but this represents less than 40 percent of all customers of REA-borrowers; the rest are non-farm residences, industrial plants, business firms, schools and churches.

This has been accomplished by loans totaling $4.68 billion through fiscal 1962, and by direct appropriations ascribed to the administrative costs of the electrification program totaling $154 million. As of June 30, 1962, total repayments of electrification loans amounted to $1.097 million and interest collected totaled $532 million. (To this should be added the parallel data on the rural telephone program—from 1950 through fiscal 1962: $909 million in loans to 790 borrowers, with $44 million of principal repaid and interest paid, $37 million. REA-borrowers serve 1,295,000 customers, over 293,000 miles of line.)

The Costs of REA

The cost of the REA program is, in part, a matter of conjecture as it involves an estimate of tax and interest revenues foregone as well as a summation of dollars directly appropriated. Subsidy features of the rural electrification program include: appropriations for administrative costs; loans of federal funds at less than their cost to the Treasury; exemption of the cooperatives from the payment of federal income taxes; tax advantages granted by some states to the cooperatives; preference rights to federal power at rates which may reflect considerable subsidies; and power contracts with private companies at rates lower than those charged other users of comparable blocks of power.

In 1955, the Hoover Commission reported as follows on the Rural Electrification Administration:

> The financial setup of the cooperatives does not make adequate provision for such rates for power or telephone service to enable them adequately to build up reserves and provide for extension or replacements.
>
> Under this method of financing, the Government has subsidized the sale of electric power to the members of the cooperative associations at considerably less than its economic cost, the subsidies being provided in the following ways:
>
> (1) The charging of interest at 2 per cent per annum, which is about one percentage point less than the interest which the Treasury must pay on long-term issues to provide the money.
>
> (2) The granting of the 5-year moratorium period with a delayed payment of interest which results in an effective rate of return of even less than 2 per cent.
>
> (3) Granting exemption from all Federal taxes (in some states these bodies are exempt from all or some local taxes).
>
> (4) Providing the administrative expenses which in the past five years have averaged about $7,750,000 annually from Federal funds.[1]

Estimates prepared for the Joint Economic Committee of the Congress show a realized cost of $251.7 million for REA's lending programs (electric and telephone combined) through fiscal 1959. To this cost must be added direct appropriations for the agency's salaries and expenses.[2]

Table XI represents an estimate of the total cost to the Federal Government of the rural electrification program. Even if REA were to collect today the $2.8 billion outstanding at the end of the 1961 fiscal year and remit this to the Treasury, the nation's taxpayers would still have spent some $370 million on the program.

---

[1] 84th Congress, 1st Session, House Document No. 107, *Lending Agencies*, pp. 74-75.

[2] 86th Congress, Joint Committee Print, *Subsidy and Subsidylike Programs of the U.S. Government*, Materials Prepared for the Joint Economic Committee, pp. 28-29.

Table XI
ESTIMATED COST TO THE FEDERAL GOVERNMENT OF THE RURAL ELECTRIFICATION PROGRAM
(in millions of dollars)

Fiscal Year	Advanced funds	Principal collections a	Funds outstanding	Average funds outstanding	Annual interest rate on marketable treasury issues b	Interest on avg. funds outstanding	Interest collected a	Average interest deficiency	Adm. funds obligated c	Annual cost of REA to federal gov't	Cumulative cost of REA to federal gov't
1961	$183.5	$100.9	$2789.8	$2748.5	3.063%	$84.19	$52.8	$31.39	$4.94	$36.33	$370.21
1960	223.6d	100.2e	2707.2	2645.5	3.499f	91.25	49.0	42.25	4.72	46.97	333.88
1959	211.8	99.9	2588.8	2527.8	2.891	73.08	45.0	28.08	4.75	32.83	286.91
1958	205.3	97.2	2471.9	2417.8	2.546	61.56	42.5	19.06	4.54	23.60	254.08
1957	186.0	84.3	2363.8	2313.0	2.707	62.61	39.4	23.21	4.27	27.48	230.48
1956	154.7	79.8	2262.1	2224.6	2.427	53.99	36.8	17.19	4.35	21.54	203.00
1955	156.7	74.4	2187.2	2146.0	2.079	44.62	32.0	12.62	4.24	16.86	181.46
1954	181.6	59.0	2104.9	2043.6	2.043	41.75	26.2	15.55	4.51	20.06	164.60
1953	207.6	48.8	1982.3	1902.9	2.207	42.00	20.3	21.70	5.72	27.42	144.54
1952	227.6	48.4	1823.5	1733.9	2.051	35.56	17.3	18.26	6.63	24.89	117.12
1951	268.1	37.2	1644.3	1528.8	1.981	30.29	14.8	15.49	7.02	22.58	92.23
1950	286.7	26.7	1413.4	1283.4	1.958	25.13	13.8	11.33	6.69	18.02	69.72
1949	321.3	22.7	1153.4	1003.1	2.001	20.07	12.7	7.37	5.97	13.34	51.70
1948	246.2	21.2	854.8	742.3	1.942	14.42	9.7	4.72	4.82	9.54	38.36
1947	190.1	13.6	629.8	541.6	1.871	10.13	8.9	1.23	5.53	6.76	28.82
1946	87.2	11.0	453.3	415.2	1.773	7.36	9.3	(1.94)	5.47	2.53	22.06
1945	39.8	10.7	377.1	362.5	1.718	6.23	8.9	(2.67)	2.90	.23	19.53
1944	18.4	15.1	348.0	346.3	1.725	5.97	11.2	(5.23)	2.55	(2.68)	19.30
1943	14.6	12.1	344.7	343.4	1.822	6.26	11.0	(4.76)	3.32	(1.44)	21.98
1942	58.2	5.5	342.2	315.8	2.225	7.03	3.6	3.43	3.85	7.28	23.42
1941	75.1	5.3	289.5	254.6	2.413	6.14	3.9	2.24	3.55	5.79	16.14
1940	99.0	1.2	219.7	170.8	2.492	4.26	4.4	(.14)	2.71	2.57	10.35
1939	62.3	.4	121.9	91.0	2.525	2.30	2.2	1.20	2.36	3.56	7.78
1938	48.1	....	60.0	36.0	2.521	.91	.2	.71	1.47	2.18	4.22
1937	11.1	....	11.9	6.4	2.525	.16	....	.16	1.19	1.35	2.04
1936	.8	....	.8	.8	2.530	.02	....	.02	.67	.69	.69

a U. S. Department of Agriculture, Rural Electrification Administration, *Rural Lines, USA. The Story of the Rural Electrification Administration's First Twenty-Five Years, 1935-1960*, Miscellaneous Publication No. 811, p. 56.

b Nelson, Paul, and Cochran, Clay L., "What About REA Interest Rate?" *Rural Electrification Education Series 22* (Washington: National Rural Electric Cooperative Association, 1939-1957), Appendix C, p. 14.

Anderson, Jerry L., Editor, *Rural Electric Fact Book* (Washington: National Rural Electric Cooperative Association, 1960), Table 16, p. 30.

c U. S. Department of Agriculture, *Report of the Administrator of the Rural Electrification Administration for 1950-61*; 85th Congress, 2d Session, Senate Hearings on Agricultural Appropriations for 1959.

d U. S. Department of Agriculture, *Report of the Administrator of the Rural Electrification Administration*, 1961, p. 2.

e Ibid., p. 4.

f U. S. Treasury Department, *Treasury Bulletin*, June 1962, Table 2, p. 22.

Financial Accomplishments

Looking next at the instrumentalities established by REA to carry electricity to the farms, the question arises: what success have they had in providing a commodity at a price, acceptable to the public, that would return total cost?

Table XII presents the composite revenues and expenses reported by REA-borrowers for the years 1952-60. Operating revenues increased by 106.5 percent while operating expenses increased by 104.6 percent, with a resulting increase in the operating margin of 115.5 percent. Clearly, the 267.6 percent increase in net profits was the result of factors other than improved operating efficiency, two in particular: (1) the non-operating margin increased from $1.255 million to $13.661 million or more than ten times; (2) the 41.9 percent increase in interest on long-term debt was substantially less than proportional to the increase in revenues or in other costs. These relationships are brought out more clearly by calculating the annual return, before interest deduction, on total depreciated assets. For these nine years, the average return was just 3.7 percent. During these same years, the Federal Government spent some $241.7 million, not counting recoverable loans, in direct subsidy of the rural electrification program. Of more significance than the total federal cost is the trend of this cost—from $24.9 million in 1952 to $47 million in 1960. It would seem that the greater the apparent prosperity of the program, the more costly it is to the Federal Government and thus to the general public.

Justification for the continuation or expansion of any business activity necessarily runs in terms of the return on total resources utilized. For maximum social benefit to be approached, resources should be attracted into those activities yielding the greatest return, and resources should be withdrawn from those activities with a low yield. If the return is just "middling," then resources will tend to be retained in that activity, neither increasing nor decreasing in amount.

In Table XIII, the composite expenses reported by REA-borrowers, 1952-60, have been deliberately increased by adding on two costs borne *for* them by various governmental units, to derive an approximate total cost of providing service: (1) ap-

Table XII
Composite Revenues and Expenses Reported by REA-Borrowers
Calendar Years 1952-60
(in thousands of dollars)

	1960	1959	1958	1957	1956	1955	1954	1953	1952	Totals
Operating revenue	$ 663,789	$ 617,780	$ 563,204	$ 523,783	$ 491,185	$ 449,626	$ 408,145	$ 362,977	$ 321,407	$4,401,846
Operating deductions:										
Cost of power	$ 246,137	$ 226,295	$ 202,693	$ 186,005	$ 171,115	$ 154,341	$ 138,237	$ 121,927	$ 106,417	$1,553,167
Distribution	71,003	63,326	59,333	56,417	51,460	48,063	46,822	43,069	38,618	478,111
Consumers accounting and collection	22,226	20,668	19,231	17,784	16,551	15,312	14,512	13,569	12,528	152,381
Administration and general	57,997	53,001	47,852	43,740	39,923	37,157	34,320	32,460	28,792	375,242
Sales promotion	11,126	10,002	8,770	7,449	6,160	5,126	4,639	4,434	3,942	61,648
Depreciation	107,878	100,527	94,530	89,573	84,306	79,597	75,776	70,091	63,347	765,625
Amortization of intangibles	1,145	1,228	1,458	1,259	1,211	1,087	1,149	992	842	10,371
Taxes	21,477	18,771	16,656	15,256	13,686	12,717	11,414	10,112	8,997	129,086
Total operating deductions	$ 538,989	$ 493,818	$ 450,523	$ 417,483	$ 384,412	$ 353,400	$ 326,869	$ 296,654	$ 263,483	$3,525,631
Operating margin	$ 124,800	$ 123,911	$ 112,681	$ 106,298	$ 106,773	$ 96,225	$ 81,276	$ 66,323	$ 57,924	$ 876,215
Non-operating margin	13,661	11,445	9,580	7,937	6,395	5,101	3,280	2,219	1,255	60,873
Total margin	$ 138,461	$ 135,356	$ 122,261	$ 114,235	$ 113,168	$ 101,326	$ 84,556	$ 68,542	$ 59,179	$ 937,088
Interest on long-term debt	$ 50,939	$ 48,702	$ 46,815	$ 45,283	$ 43,561	$ 42,339	$ 40,397	$ 38,061	$ 35,195	$ 391,292
Other deductions	1,029	660	582	511	659	512	537	486	455	5,431
Total deductions	$ 51,968	$ 49,362	$ 47,397	$ 45,794	$ 44,220	$ 42,851	$ 40,934	$ 38,547	$ 35,650	$ 396,723
Net profit	$ 86,493	$ 85,994	$ 74,864	$ 68,441	$ 68,948	$ 58,475	$ 43,662	$ 29,995	$ 23,529	$ 540,361
Interest charged to construction	719	361	443	459	354	807	344	832	1,018	5,337
Net margin reported	$ 87,212	$ 86,355	$ 75,307	$ 68,900	$ 69,302	$ 59,282	$ 44,006	$ 30,827	$ 24,547	$ 545,698
Total assets, 12/31	$3,508,977	$3,325,943	$3,109,511	$2,941,646	$2,773,760	$2,612,994	$2,460,409	$2,295,703	$2,107,510	$25,136,453
Return on total assets (Net Profit plus Interest) (Total Assets)	3.9%	4.0%	3.9%	3.9%	4.1%	3.9%	3.4%	3.0%	2.8%	3.7%

Source: U. S. Department of Agriculture, Rural Electrification Administration, *Annual Statistical Report, 1952-1960*, REA Bulletin 1-1.

Table XIII

COMPOSITE REVENUES AND EXPENSES REPORTED BY REA-BORROWERS[a]
ADJUSTED FOR FEDERAL INTEREST AND FEDERAL ADMINISTRATION SUBSIDIES AND
FOR STATE SUBSIDIES,[e] CALENDAR YEARS
(in thousands of dollars)

	1960	1959	1958	1957	1956	1955	1954	1953	1952	1952-60 totals
Revenues:										
Operating revenues	$ 663,789	$ 617,730	$ 563,204	$ 523,783	$ 491,185	$ 449,626	$ 408,145	$ 362,977	$ 321,407	$4,401,846
Non-operating margin	13,661	11,445	9,580	7,937	6,395	5,101	3,280	2,219	1,255	60,873
Total revenue	$ 677,450	$ 629,175	$ 572,784	$ 531,720	$ 497,580	$ 454,727	$ 411,425	$ 365,196	$ 322,662	$4,462,719
Total expense deductions:										
Cost of power	$ 246,137	$ 226,295	$ 202,693	$ 186,005	$ 171,115	$ 154,341	$ 138,237	$ 121,927	$ 106,417	$1,553,167
Distribution	71,003	63,326	59,333	56,417	51,460	48,063	46,822	43,069	38,618	478,111
Consumers accounting and collection	22,226	20,668	19,231	17,784	16,551	15,312	14,512	13,569	12,528	152,381
Administration and general	57,997	53,001	47,852	43,740	39,923	37,157	34,320	32,460	28,792	375,242
Sales promotion	11,126	10,002	8,770	7,449	6,160	5,126	4,639	4,434	3,942	61,648
Depreciation	107,878	100,527	94,530	89,573	84,306	79,597	75,776	70,091	63,347	765,625
Amortization of intangibles	1,145	1,228	1,458	1,259	1,211	1,087	1,149	992	842	10,371
Taxes	21,477	18,771	16,656	15,256	13,686	12,717	11,414	10,112	8,997	129,086
REA administrative allocation[b]	4,717	4,751	4,541	4,268	4,346	4,244	4,505	5,722	6,631	43,725
Tax adjustment[c]	63,181	61,397	54,705	52,040	49,648	45,908	41,959	33,143	31,288	433,269
Other deductions	1,029	660	582	511	659	512	537	486	455	5,431
Total expense	$ 607,916	$ 560,626	$510,351	$ 474,302	$ 439,065	$ 404,064	$ 373,870	$ 336,005	$ 301,857	$4,008,056
Net profit	$ 69,534	$ 68,549	$ 62,433	$ 57,418	$ 58,515	$ 50,663	$ 37,555	$ 29,191	$ 20,805	$ 454,663
Less interest on long-term debt	$ 50,939	$ 48,702	$ 46,815	$ 45,283	$ 43,561	$ 42,339	$ 40,397	$ 38,061	$ 35,195	$ 391,292
Interest adjustment[d]	39,940	23,023	13,497	16,711	9,659	1,728	905	4,103	930	110,496
Total cost of money	$ 90,879	$ 71,725	$ 60,312	$ 61,994	$ 53,220	$ 44,067	$ 41,302	$ 42,164	$ 36,125	$ 501,788
Profit available to owners (*deficit)	*$ 21,345	$ 3,176	*$ 2,121	$ 4,576	$ 5,295	$ 6,596	*$ 3,747	*$ 12,973	*$ 15,320	$ 47,125
Interest charged to construction	719	807	354	459	443	361	344	832	1,018	5,337
Increase (*decrease) owners investment	*$ 20,626	$ 2,369	$ 2,475	$ 4,117	$ 5,738	$ 6,957	*$ 3,403	*$ 12,141	*$ 14,302	*$ 41,788
Net assets end of year[a]	$3,508,977	$3,325,943	$3,109,511	$2,941,646	$2,773,760	$2,612,994	$2,460,409	$2,295,703	$2,107,512	$25,136,455
Net profit ÷ Net assets	2.0%	2.0%	2.0%	2.0%	2.1%	1.9%	1.5%	1.3%	1.0%	1.8%

a U. S. Department of Agriculture, Rural Electrification Administration, "Rural Electrification Borrowers," *Annual Statistical Report, 1952-1960*, REA Bulletin 1-1.

b Estimated from U. S. Department of Agriculture, *Report of the Administrator of the Rural Electrification Administration, 1960*, Table 22, p. 31.

c Edison Electric Institute, *Statistical Yearbook of the Electric Utility Industry for 1960*, pp. 60-61, tax adjustment obtained by determining the relationship between gross plant and taxes, other than federal income for class A and B, privately-owned electric utilities; Federal Power Commission, *Statistics of Electric Utilities in the United States, 1960, Privately Owned*, FPC S-151, pp. 27-29.

d The interest adjustment is the excess of average cost to the Federal Government over the 2 percent rate charged to REA.

e No adjustment for federal income taxes since the program overall has not been profitable.

propriations for administrative costs of REA's electrification activities; and (2) an increase in taxes, other than federal income, to the same relative amount as that borne by private electric companies. With these two adjustments, the yield on resources employed averaged just 1.8 percent and ranged from a low of 1 percent in 1952 to a high of 2.1 percent in 1956.

In six of these nine years, REA-borrowers were unable to earn enough, after taxes equal to those paid by private utilities, to repay the Federal Government a sum equal to the average cost of money to the Treasury. Quite obviously, the contention of the rural cooperatives that any increase in the interest rate would drive them out of business, with their present pricing policy, is well taken.[3] But to the question of charging a full-cost price instead, no really satisfactory answer has been given.

Yet another way to measure the efficiency of REA-borrowers is presented in Table XIV. The operating achievements of the cooperatives, before tax and interest costs, are compared with the same data for Class A and B Private Utilities for the years 1956-60. The total costs of REA-borrowers increased by 39 percent, along with an increase in total revenues of 36 percent. In contrast, the total costs of the private companies increased by 29 percent, total revenues by 31 percent. The margin available for payments of taxes, interest, and dividends, and to support company growth, increased by 25 percent for REA-borrowers and by 35 percent for the private companies. REA-borrowers' earnings before taxes and interest ranged between 4.2 percent and 4.8 percent of net assets. The private companies' earnings before taxes and interest ranged between 10.6 and 11.2 percent of net assets.

Interest costs reported by REA-borrowers amounted to 1.8 percent of year-end debt in each of these five years, while their debt burden declined from 85.2 to 78.6 percent of net assets. Interest costs reported by the private companies grew from 3.2 to 3.6 percent of year-end debt during these five years, and their debt burden increased from 45.7 to 46.9 percent of net assets. If all these borrowers were obtaining funds in the competitive market, it is probable that the cooperatives—with their higher

[3] NRECA, *Rural Electric Fact Book*, p. 29.

Table XIV

OPERATING DATA OF REA-BORROWERS AND CLASS A AND B PRIVATE ELECTRIC UTILITIES, 1956-60
(in thousands of dollars)

	1960 Operating results		1959 Operating results		1958 Operating results		1957 Operating results		1956 Operating results	
	REA-borrowers	Class A & B private utilities	REA-borrowers	Class A & B private utilities	REA-borrowers	Class A & B private utilities	REA-borrowers	Class A & B private utilities	REA-borrowers	Class A & B private utilities
Revenues:										
Operating revenues	$ 663,789	$11,919,501	$ 617,730	$11,128,972	$ 563,204	$10,194,819	$ 523,783	$9,670,378	$ 491,185	$9,053,731
Non-operating revenues	13,661	81,067	11,445	66,121	9,580	60,441	7,937	67,057	6,395	63,518
Total revenues	$ 677,450	$12,000,568	$ 629,175	$11,195,093	$ 572,784	$10,255,260	$ 531,720	$9,737,435	$ 497,580	$9,117,249
Less costs of operation:										
Operating deductions other than taxes	$ 517,512	$6,959,536	$ 475,048	$6,497,897	$ 433,867	$6,030,286	$ 402,229	$5,782,395	$ 370,726	$5,365,931
REA administrative allocation	4,717	....	4,751	....	4,541	....	4,268	....	4,346	....
Other deductions	1,029	26,365	660	31,889	582	35,062	511	28,620	659	32,305
Total deductions	$ 523,258	$6,985,901	$ 480,459	$6,529,786	$ 438,990	$6,065,348	$ 407,008	$5,811,015	$ 375,731	$5,398,236
Return available for taxes, interest, and other investors	$ 154,192	$5,014,667	$ 148,716	$4,665,307	$ 133,794	$4,189,912	$ 124,712	$3,926,420	$ 121,849	$3,719,013
Net assets end of year	$3,508,977	$44,855,678	$3,325,943	$42,212,273	$3,109,511	$39,384,435	$2,941,646	$36,497,588	$2,773,760	$33,341,279
Rate of return on total resources	4.4%	11.2%	4.8%	11.1%	4.3%	10.6%	4.2%	10.8%	4.4%	11.2%
Return on total resources	$ 154,192	$5,014,667	$ 148,716	$4,665,307	$ 133,794	$4,189,912	$ 124,712	$3,926,420	$ 121,849	$3,719,013
Interest recorded	50,939	766,110	48,702	701,083	46,815	641,616	45,283	558,224	43,561	492,947
Taxes recorded	21,477	2,372,680	18,771	2,197,982	16,656	1,928,744	15,256	1,832,034	13,686	1,758,403
Interest as percent of year-end debt	1.8%	3.6%	1.8%	3.5%	1.8%	3.5%	1.8%	3.3%	1.8%	3.2%
Taxes as percent of total assets	0.6%	5.2%	0.6%	5.2%	0.5%	4.9%	0.5%	5.0%	0.5%	5.3%
Taxes as percent of total revenue	3.2%	19.8%	3.0%	19.6%	2.9%	18.8%	2.9%	18.8%	2.8%	19.3%
Long-term debt	$2,756,359	$21,056,816	$2,663,874	$19,833,915	$2,542,769	$18,578,842	$2,456,254	$17,050,875	$2,362,272	$15,231,199
Long-term debt ÷ net assets	78.6%	46.9%	80.1%	47.0%	81.8%	47.2%	83.5%	46.7%	85.2%	45.7%

Source: Federal Power Commission, *Statistics of Electric Utilities in the United States, 1960, Privately Owned,* FPC S-151, pp. 27-29; U. S. Department of Agriculture, REA Bulletin 1-1, *1960 Annual Statistical Report,* pp. 12-13; U. S. Department of Agriculture, *Report of the Administrator of the Rural Electrification Administration, 1960,* Table 22, p. 31.

debt ratio—would have interest costs considerably higher than comparable private companies. It is thus apparent that the Federal Government has subsidized the cooperatives not only directly, by paying some of their interest costs, but also indirectly by substituting its credit standing for that of the cooperatives. This represents, for the co-ops, a substantial competitive advantage. It grants them a uniquely privileged position in the capital investment market.

Taxes reported by the cooperatives increased from one-half of 1 percent of net assets in 1956 to six-tenths of 1 percent in 1960. Omitting deferred federal income taxes, other taxes reported by the private utilities declined from 5.3 percent of net assets in 1956 to 5.2 percent in 1960. In relation to total revenues, taxes reported by cooperatives rose from 2.8 percent in 1956 to 3.2 percent in 1960. Taxes paid by the private utilities rose from 19.3 percent of total revenues in 1956 to 19.8 percent in 1960.

Even these results are considerably inflated, moreover, since the cooperatives obtain more than 45 percent of their power from federal and other public suppliers whose rates do not cover the full cost of service.[4] With costs thus understated and profits overstated, REA-borrowers still have not presented a very favorable record.

If the measure of success is the ability to earn a return, on total resources employed, sufficient to pay the competitive cost of money and a proportionate share of the costs of government at all levels, then REA-borrowers have not even begun to make their own way.

The recommendations of the Hoover Commission are worth repeating:

> In view of the great advance made in farm electrification, it is our belief that the time has arrived for the reorganization of the Rural

[4] *Audit of Southeastern Power System and Southeastern Power Administration,* Fiscal years 1959 and 1960, by Comptroller General of the United States, p. 5.

Audit of Arkansas, White, and Red River Basins Water Resources Development Program and Southwestern Power Administration, Fiscal year 1957, by the Comptroller General of the United States, pp. 3-4.

Edison Electric Institute, *A Study of the TVA Power Business,* 1960.

Electrification Administration into a self-supporting institution securing its own financing from private sources.[5]

In spite of their inadequate return on total assets, REA-subsidized cooperatives were supplying power to residential customers at rates 5 percent lower than those of private companies in 1960.[6]

The economic conditions that may once have justified this expenditure of large sums of public money, as a subsidy to rural residents and business establishments, no longer exist. Subsidies, direct and indirect, could be reduced gradually until they no longer constitute a burden on the American taxpayer. The rural electric cooperative, and its customers, should be encouraged to accept full responsibility for its financial viability in providing a wanted service at a fair price, adequate to compensate the suppliers of capital and to pay the costs of government services received.

Senator Dominick, in proposing that REA interest rates be pegged to the costs of current Treasury borrowings, has admirably summed up the questions raised by REA's present status and by its future prospects:

> . . . I am not unmindful that REA has often been referred to as a "congressional sacred cow." . . . However, I believe a realistic assessment of the program under present day circumstances and policies will show the need for change. I certainly have no quarrel with the accomplishments of REA in bringing low cost electricity to American farms. This was its original objective and a fine one. However, my chief concern is: Where do we go from here? With about 98 percent of all farms presently receiving electricity, a thorough and searching examination of the Rural Electrification Administration is in order. It is now facing increasingly violent attacks which could destroy it unless the most glaring defect, the subsidized interest rate, is eliminated.[7]

---

[5] *Op. cit.*, pp. 75-76.
[6] REA Bulletin 1-1, *1960 Annual Statistical Report*, "Rural Electrification Borrowers," Table VIII, p. 11.
FPC S-151, *Statistics of Electric Utilities in the United States, 1960, Privately Owned*, Table 9, p. 21.
[7] *Congressional Record*, July 10, 1963, p. 11675.

SUMMARY AND CONCLUSIONS

(1) From its inception in 1935 and its statutory establishment a year later, REA has had one explicit purpose, and one
only: to bring electricity to the nation's farms. About 98 percent of all farms now receive central-station service—over half
of them from REA-borrowers.

(2) Furthermore, coincident with REA's tenure, the total
number of farms has steadily declined while net farm income
has increased. Today, REA's program is oriented not primarily
toward agriculture but rather toward the rural non-farm sector
and toward suburban areas, both residential and industrial,

70

within metropolitan complexes. REA's policy seems to be to compete aggressively for consumers in such areas, which now constitute fully 75 percent of all new customers added by REA-borrowers.

(3) Now that the task for which REA was created has been carried out, its continuing and changing functions and objectives could well be subjected to a searching reappraisal. At the present time, through its own directives and promotional activities, REA is in effect re-writing its own statutory authorization— by what some have called "backdoor lawmaking."

(4) Considered purely as economic enterprises, within the context of a freely competitive market, the rural cooperatives have demonstrated insufficient efficiency to justify their continued support at public expense.

(5) Despite long-term loans in excess of $4.6 billion at interest rates pegged to an artificial 2 percent, the provision of free administrative services, and exemption from nearly all federal and state taxes, REA-borrowers are not yet earning a return adequate to repay the Treasury the full cost of its own borrowings or to assume a proportionate share of local, state, and federal taxes.

(6) At the present time, these special advantages constitute a subsidy to residents, commercial firms, and industries in the nation's rural non-farm areas.

(7) The rural electric co-ops should price their product so as to become self-sufficient business enterprises, in fair competition with private power companies.

(8) The new and growing emphasis on generation-and-transmission loans also deserves careful appraisal, especially since such loans permit REA-borrowers—operating as privileged tax-exempt islands — to prevent the operation of privately-owned taxpaying facilities.

(9) The triple criteria for granting G and T loans—availability of power, cost of power, and the nebulous concept "security of the cooperative system"—should be subjected to congressional examination and then, if approved, should be specifically authorized.

(10) The present "secrecy policy" surrounding contracts executed between rural co-ops and REA, and subject only to REA discretion, prevents systematic evaluation of the justification for such large-scale use of public funds.

PUBLICATIONS

STUDIES

The Economic Analysis of Labor Union Power, Revised Edition, *Edward H. Chamberlin*—1963

United States Aid to Yugoslavia and Poland—Analysis of a Controversy, *Milorad M. Drachkovitch*—1963

Communists in Coalition Governments, *Gerhart Niemeyer*—1963

Subsidized Food Consumption, *Don Paarlberg*—1963

Automation—The Impact of Technological Change, *Yale Brozen*—1963

Essay on Apportionment and Representative Government, *Alfred de Grazia*—1963 ($2.00)

American Foreign Aid Doctrines, *Edward C. Banfield*—1963

The Rescue of the Dollar, *Wilson E. Schmidt*—1963

The Role of Gold, *Arthur Kemp*—1963

Pricing Power and "Administrative" Inflation—Concepts, Facts and Policy Implications, *Henry W. Briefs*—1962

Depreciation Reform and Capital Replacement, *William T. Hogan*—1962

The Federal Antitrust Laws, *Jerrold G. Van Cise*—1962

Consolidated Grants: A Means of Maintaining Fiscal Responsibility, *George C. S. Benson* and *Harold F. McClelland*—1961

Inflation: Its Causes and Cures, Revised and Enlarged Edition, *Gottfried Haberler*—1961

The Patchwork History of Foreign Aid, *Lorna Morley* and *Felix Morley*—1961

U.S. Immigration Policy and

World Population Problems, *Virgil Salera*—1960

*Inflation: Its Causes and Cures, *Gottfried Haberler*—1960

Voluntary Health Insurance in the United States, *Rita R. Campbell* and *W. Glenn Campbell*—1960

Unionism Reappraised: From Classical Unionism to Union Establishment, *Goetz Briefs*—1960

United States Aid and Indian Economic Development, *P. T. Bauer*—1959

Improving National Transportation Policy, *John H. Frederick*—1959

The Question of Governmental Oil Import Restrictions, *William H. Peterson*—1959

Labor Unions and the Concept of Public Service, *Roscoe Pound*—1959

Labor Unions and Public Policy, *Edward H. Chamberlin, Philip D. Bradley, Gerard D. Reilly,* and *Roscoe Pound*—1958. 177 pp. ($4.50)

National Aid to Higher Education, *George C. S. Benson* and *John M. Payne*—1958

Agricultural Surpluses and Export Policy, *Raymond F. Mikesell*—1958

The Economic Analysis of Labor Union Power, *Edward H. Chamberlin*—1958

Post-War West German and United Kingdom Recovery, *David McCord Wright*—1957

The Regulation of Natural Gas, *James W. McKie*—1957

---

*Out of Print

73

Legal Immunities of Labor Unions, *Roscoe Pound*—1957

*Automation—Its Impact on Economic Growth and Stability, *Almarin Phillips*—1957

*Involuntary Participation In Unionism, *Philip D. Bradley*—1956

The Role of Government in Developing Peaceful Uses of Atomic Energy, *Arthur Kemp*—1956

The Role of The Federal Government in Housing, *Paul F. Wendt*—1956

The Upper Colorado Reclamation Project, Pro by *Sen. Arthur V. Watkins*, Con by *Raymond Moley*—1956

*Federal Aid to Education—Boon or Bane? *Roger A. Freeman*—1955

States Rights and the Law of Labor Relations, *Gerard D. Reilly*—1955

Three Taft-Hartley Issues: Secondary Boycotts, "Mandatory" Injunctions, Replaced Strikers' Votes, *Theodore R. Iserman*—1955

What Price Federal Reclamation? *Raymond Moley*—1955

Private Investments Abroad, *Charles R. Carroll*—1954

Farm Price Supports—Rigid or Flexible, *Karl Brandt*—1954

*Currency Convertibility, *Gottfried Haberler*—1954

The Control of the Location of Industry in Great Britain, *John Jewkes*—1952

The Walsh-Healey Public Contracts Act, *John V. Van Sickle*—1952

The Economics of Full Employment: An Analysis of the U.N. Report on National and International Measures for Full Employment, *Wilhelm Röpke*—1952

Price Fixing for Foodstuffs, *Earl L. Butz*—1951

Manpower Needs and the Labor Supply, *Clarence D. Long*—1951

An Economic Approach to Antitrust Problems, *Clare E. Griffin*—1951 ($1.00)

*Valley Authorities, *Raymond Moley*—1950

*Farm Price and Income Supports, *O. B. Jesness*—1950

*Monetary Policy and Economic Prosperity: Testimony of Dr. W. W. Stewart (July 3-4, 1930) before the Macmillan Committee with introduction by *Donald B. Woodward*—1950

Corporate Profits in Perspective, *John Linter*—1949

*Current Problems of Immigration Policy, *E. P. Hutchinson*—1949

Guaranteed Employment and Wage Plans. A Summary and Critique of the Latimer Report and Related Documents, *William A. Berridge* and *Cedric Wolfe*—1948

The Foreign Loan Policy of the United States, *J. B. Condliffe*—1947

*Proposals for Consideration by an International Conference on Trade and Employment, *J. B. Condliffe*—1946

The Market for Risk Capital, *Jules I. Bogen*—1946

Unless otherwise shown in listing, Studies 1953 and earlier, 50 cents each; 1954 to date, $1.00 each.

LEGISLATIVE AND SPECIAL ANALYSES
87th Congress, Second Session, 1962

No. 1—The Proposal to Increase the National Debt Ceiling

No. 2—Reorganization Plan No. 1, of 1962 to Create a Department of Urban Affairs and Housing

No. 3—Foreign Trade: Part I: The Operation, Administration, and Development of the Trade Agreements Program. *A Special Analysis*

No. 4—Foreign Trade: Part II: Economic Consequences of Trade Liberalization. *A Special Analysis*

No. 5—Foreign Trade: Part III: Import Adjustment Assistance and Alternatives. *A Special Analysis*

No. 6—Foreign Trade: Part IV: The European Economic Community (Common Market). *A Special Analysis*

No. 7—Purchase of United Nations Bonds. Bill by *Sen. Sparkman*

No. 8—Foreign Trade: Part V:

Proposals to Amend and Extend the Reciprocal Trade Agreements Legislation. *A Special Analysis*

No. 9—Proposals to Provide Health Care for the Aged Under Social Security. Bills by *Sen. Anderson, et al.; Rep. King*

No. 10—Tax Proposals Relating to Foreign Income. Bill by *Rep. Mills*

No. 11—Public Welfare Amendments of 1962. Bill by *Rep. Mills*

No. 12—The Drug Control Bills and Other Proposals to Amend the Food, Drug and Cosmetic Act. Bills by *Sen. Kefauver; Reps. Sullivan, Celler* and *Harris*

No. 13—The Proposed International Coffee Agreement. *A Special Analysis*

No. 14—The Pacific Northwest Power Preference Bills. Bills by *Sen. Anderson; Reps. Hansen* and *Pfost*

88th Congress, First Session, 1963

No. 1—History and Powers of the House Committee on Rules. *A Special Analysis*

No. 2—The Youth Employment Bill. Bills by *Sen. Humphrey; Rep. Perkins*

No. 3—Tax Proposals and the Federal Finances: Part I: Federal Expenditures. *A Special Analysis*

No. 4—Tax Proposals and the Federal Finances: Part II: The American Tax System: Background for

Studying Proposals for Change. *A Special Analysis*

No. 5—Proposals to Increase the National Debt Ceiling. Bill by *Rep. Mills*

No. 6—Area Redevelopment Act Amendments of 1963. Bills by *Sen. Douglas and others; Rep. Patman*

No. 7—Tax Proposals and the Federal Finances: Part III: Tax Issues of 1963. *A Special Analysis*

---

* Out of Print

Single Copy One Dollar